The Swing Trader's Bible

Founded in 1807, John Wiley & Sons is the oldest independent publishing company in the United States. With offices in North America, Europe, Australia and Asia, Wiley is globally committed to developing and marketing print and electronic products and services for our customers' professional and personal knowledge and understanding.

The Wiley Trading series features books by traders who have survived the market's ever changing temperament and have prospered—some by reinventing systems, others by getting back to basics. Whether a novice trader, professional or somewhere in-between, these books will provide the advice and strategies needed to prosper today and well into the future.

For a list of available titles, please visit our Web site at www.Wiley Finance.com.

The Swing Trader's Bible

Strategies to Profit from Market Volatility

MATTHEW McCALL

MARK WHISTLER

WILEY

John Wiley & Sons, Inc.

Published by John Wiley & Sons, Inc., Hoboken, New Jersey.
Published simultaneously in Canada.

For general information on our other products and services or for technical support, please contact our Customer Care Department within the United States at (800) 762-2974, outside the United States at (317) 572-3993 or fax (317) 572-4002.

Wiley also publishes its books in a variety of electronic formats. Some content that appears in print may not be available in electronic books. For more information about Wiley products, visit our web site at www.wiley.com.

Library of Congress Cataloging-in-Publication Data:

McCall, Matthew, 1976–
   The swing trader's bible : strategies to profit from market volatility/
Matthew McCall, Mark Whistler.
        p. cm. – (Wiley trading series)
   Includes bibliographical references and indexes.
   ISBN 978-0-470-30826-4 (cloth)
 1. Investment analysis.   2. Portfolio management.   3. Stocks.   I. Whistler,
Mark.   II. Title.
   HG4529.M383 2009
   332.64–dc22

                                                              2008028073

Printed in the United States of America.

10   9   8   7   6   5   4   3   2   1

Contents

Acknowledgments

T hank you so much to Kevin Commins, Meg Freeborn, Pamela van Giessen, and John Wiley & Sons, Inc., for making this book possible. Also, thank you to Sandy Whistler and Ed Juhan for being incredible parents and to Karen, Mike, and Ryan Eck; Paul, Lauren, and Alexis Whistler; and Eddie Kwong, Larry Connors, Danilo Torres, Nick Collard, and the rest of the TradingMarkets.com team. All have helped make this book possible in some form or another.

Thank you to Leigh Stevens; even the third book is due to your help from the start.

Preface

T rading and investing are among the most exciting and rewarding pursuits around, there's no doubt about it. Where else can you make all of your dreams come true, while having direct control over every step of your fate? Not too many places. However, trading and investing provide one of those special situations, where with enough hard work and understanding, all of our futures can become as bright as our most vivid dreams of greatness. It's not easy, though, investing in financial markets. After all, anytime there's money on the line for almost anything in this world, emotions come into play as well.

However, with a solid repertoire of proven tools, there's no mountain any of us can't scale. With this in mind, *The Swing Trader's Bible* is many years of culled experience between us—both of whom work within financial markets professionally.

Friends for many years, we wanted to create an easy-to-read, simplified book to help investors and traders of all levels move toward profitability within the ever-changing sea of investment markets. The lessons within the very book in your hands are those of trial and error, the result of many years of hard work.

We are proud to share with you the trading strategies that we believe will give you the best opportunity to become successful and fulfill your dreams. A concept that resonates throughout the book is simplicity. We are not trying to reinvent the wheel or teach nuclear fusion. Our goal is to share with you strategies that can be learned through some good old-fashioned hard work.

We hope that you are able to immediately apply the strategies to your day-to-day investing. What you're reading isn't just theory by any means whatsoever. The strategies outlined in *The Swing Trader's Bible* are the same methods we use every day.

Remember, it is not easy to reach your goals as a trader; however, greatness is attainable if you have the knowledge of the right strategies.

The Swing Trader's Bible

CHAPTER 1

Determining Your Trading Style

M any investors in the market never stop to consider what type of trader they truly are. While it doesn't sound like something that would be all that important, knowing exactly what type of trader you are can make or break your investing career. Imagine the aforementioned in terms of a football team. The players are all quite talented; most can run fast, hit hard, and have the dexterous ability to throw and catch the ball. However, some are more skilled than others in certain areas. Receivers catch better than kickers; it's just part of their makeup. However, if the receiver were to attempt to do the kicker's job, most likely not many field-goal points would be scored.

Investing in the market is the same. Within your personality makeup, you are probably well suited for a particular type of trading; the only question is what type is it? In general, there are three types of traders within the market: position traders, swing traders, and day traders.

- **Position Traders:** These investors are generally the buy-and-hold type of traders who stick with their stocks over the long haul. Guys like Warren Buffett fit precisely into this category. Position traders can be both long and short; however, one theme constantly surfaces: These guys are in it for a large, long-term move. Usually, position traders only buy stocks, as over time, markets usually ascend. Take the Dow Jones Industrial Average (INDU) for example. Over the past 13 years, the Dow is up about 800 percent, something buy-and-hold investors in Dow stocks are likely to be thrilled with. Options traders can also be position traders, too, though usually they do so through covered calls, that is, attempting to lower their cost basis in select stocks, while also buying LEAP options. (See Chapter 19 for more on covered calls and LEAP options.)

- **Swing Traders:** Investors who take shorter-term positions in anticipation of quick market movements over a series of days, or weeks, generally fall into this category. Swing traders are possibly the most dynamic of the three types of traders, as they are able to switch up holding times quickly, as the market demands. Swing traders move both long and short, taking advantage of technical analysis, earnings, fundamentals, and macro market events.

- **Day Traders:** We'll call these guys the kings of stress. Day traders attempt to capitalize on intraday movements with the markets, often trading on momentum and news. Day traders sometimes become swing traders, if a position warrants holding for a longer period. Moreover, from our experiences, day traders can often become position traders, when they hold a loser for way too long! Day trading is ideal for those who are able to handle erratic market movements, while also having the time to actually monitor positions throughout the day. It's important to note that if you don't want to trade for a living, or don't have the luxury to watch your trades every moment, day trading should be left to the pros. In essence, day trading is the riskiest of all three styles, as often short-term momentum can trigger positions against the larger trend. While the same occurs in swing trading from time to time, the erratic behavior of day trading against the trend can lead to large losers, should the position turn in the wrong direction.

With these definitions in mind, note that we have compiled this book with strategies that we find really work for swing traders in almost any market environment. What's more, as you're about to see, swing trading is a much better alternative to day trading for those who are seeking slightly less stress in their lives that what day trading entails. With the proper analytics and timing, swing trading can be immensely profitable for those with patience, research, a wide variety of tools (which you'll read about here), and rock-solid money-management skills.

WHY SWING TRADING IS A BETTER ALTERNATIVE TO DAY TRADING

Day trading is, without a doubt, the toughest way of the three previously mentioned trading styles to consistently make money. However, many people are attracted to the glamour and excitement of day trading, which unfortunately hardly ever ends well, especially if the trader has no previous professional market experience. Like many things in this world, when it comes to day trading, probably only 10 percent of the people make 90 percent of the money. Fact is, most independent traders usually blow up and fade away.

I (Whistler) began my trading career on a day-trading floor in the dot.bomb era. When I started trading, there were about 25 guys on the floor, all trading breakout momentum. When I moved on to trade professionally, there were only about three or four of the original guys left. Almost all of the others lost virtually all of their money. We used to joke with one another when we'd see a new trader come in who didn't have much experience. We'd say, "Hey pal, why don't you give me half of all of your money right now and take the entire year off. You'll have more money at the end of the year, if you do." While it seemed funny at the time to see the reaction of the poor bloke attempting to break into the floor, the joke was actually the truth. Really, it wasn't funny at all.

Swing trading, on the other hand, can be a much more effective trading style, especially for newer traders. By holding positions overnight and even for a few weeks, traders can expose less money for larger moves. Think about it for a moment.

If you were to invest $10,000 in a $50.00 stock and it moved $3.00, the day trading profit would be $600. Equally, the swing trading profit would be $600 as well. However, on an intraday basis, the stock would have to move 6 percent to make the aforementioned event become a reality. However, if you were to hold that same stock for two weeks, you would only need to see the stock rise 0.006 percent per day (assuming 10-trading days), something much more feasible than the intraday move in terms of percentages.

At the end of the day, what it comes down to is the fact that by swing trading instead of day trading, investors are able to commit less capital to the markets to reach extraordinary gains. It is important to note that swing traders do take on "overnight risk," something day traders do not have. Overnight risk is the odds swing traders hold that a position gaps away from them when markets open in the morning, usually after unforeseen news. However, with the proper research, the swing trader actually seeks to make overnight gap risk another tool in their repertoire that actually helps increase their bottom line.

The question, then, is what types of strategies constantly return profits that will make investors wealthy over the long run? We are happy to tell you that *The Swing Trader's Bible* attempts to answer that question.

At the end of the day, the strategies here have helped us book profits day in and day out over the years, with significantly less stress than day trading, or than long-term buy and hold when the market upends.

It is important to reiterate one very important point. The concepts in this book have been intentionally simplified. There are plenty of complicated quant-based trading programs in the market, creating the false impression that overcomplicating the market through math is the only way to truly make money. What's more, many math-based traders often ridicule those who keep their trading simple, as there is a sense of market elitism that often comes with quant-based system traders.

I (Whistler) will tell you one thing, though. I've been on many trading floors and have personally seen some of the greatest traders at work. What I know from my years is this: some of the wealthiest traders in the world are not those who overcomplicate the market through math, fundamentals, or technicals. Truly prosperous traders—more often than not—are the people who understand the big picture, know how to keep it simple, take time to look at fundamentals, economics, and technicals, while also having a solid predetermined money-management plan in place. These supertraders have a solid sense of trading instinct, based on many years of understanding the larger dynamic ebb and flow of money in the market. Many of these guys are swing traders with one very similar trait: they know how to dissect markets, news, fundamentals, and technicals, while still keeping the information at a simple, commonsense level.

See, when we overcomplicate things, we often lose sight of common sense, something that is vital to continual profitability within the markets. I remember on the floor, some of the most profitable momentum traders would joke that they made a point to never read about the companies they traded. The philosophy was that by actually knowing what was happening on a fundamental level in the company, the trader would have an opinion about the stock and thus fail to be able to trade impartially with market momentum. We are clearly *not* recommending this strategy here but are simply pointing out something interesting. To be profitable as a swing trader, it is important to do all of our research; however, if at any point our opinions about a company or market begin to sway our common sense, it's time to take a step back and not trade. Should common sense fade because we're too close to the situation, we are unlikely to be able to make the right decisions when the heat kicks up.

Thus, always keep an open mind about the swing trading strategies presented here. The strategies do work, but they are not going to work 100 percent of the time. That's just the way it is. In the markets, nothing works all the time, and eventually every trader is going to be faced with a losing position. It's when the walls start to crumble that we earn our way, and with the strategies in this book, most traders should be able to fall back or switch methodologies to either recoup or trade out of losing positions—but only if they are strong enough to never break their money-management rules, yet also open-minded and able to switch from something that's not working to something that is.

Often, day traders don't have the same time luxury that swing traders have, and it's important for swing traders to remember that they have plenty of tools to adapt to changing market circumstances, should they be savvy enough to choose to use them. Next we'll cover what you need to know to use this book effectively and to trade profitably while living a low-stress investing life.

HOW TO SUCCESSFULLY IMPLEMENT WINNING TRADES

First and foremost, it's important to understand—and embrace—the concept that investing is not easy. If it were, everyone would be doing it. However, because it is one of the most competitive, relentless, and unforgiving methods of growing wealth, there's also another side to the coin. For those who truly understand markets and take the time to learn about investing, the profits can be staggering. Unlike owning a business, real estate, or even your career, investing has one unique advantage: you can turn it off at any moment. If a position goes against you, the trade can be closed at any moment, thus containing losses, while giving you the opportunity to look for new—and profitable—setups within the market. Yes, businesses can restructure, houses can be sold, and careers can be changed, but rarely overnight. If you remember that swing trading and investing provides you with the instant ability to change your fate, the sky will never grow dark, and should a position move against you, your losses can be shut off by simply closing the trade.

To use this book effectively, you must have solid money-management skills, and also take the time to understand investment psychology. Our emotions can easily get the best of us when a trade starts to fail; however, if we have rock-solid money-management skills in place, we can easily keep our emotions in check. It is highly recommended for investors to take the time to sit down and evaluate their money-management plans to effectively use this book. If you do, if you have a money-management plan in place before ever trading, you will be head and shoulders above many who attempt to make money in the markets. To help cover this area, we discuss money management through effectively using stop losses in Chapter 2. However, without the discipline to stick to stops (and a larger money-management plan), investors may as well toss their money on the craps table in Vegas.

To effectively use this book, swing traders also need to understand the larger paradigm of herd mentality in the market. Consider these two quotes by nineteenth-century playwright Henrik Ibsen:[1]

> *"The majority is always wrong; the minority is rarely right."*
> *"The strongest man in the world is he who stands most alone."*

These quotes tell us a few very important things. First, like Galileo proved the sun does not orbit the earth, rare individuals are able to transcend major herd market mentality, thus making major breakthroughs not only in their own lives but in society, too. However, the majority is often wrong, something we've seen time and time again in the markets, economics, society, and politics.

Just a few examples include the dot.bomb bubble of the late 1990s and the subprime real estate mess of the past few years. Fact is, whenever the herd is making money hand over fist in some area of the market or economy, be very, very afraid, because exuberance has set in, and the herd is probably about to find their rears handed to them on a silver platter. Then, the blame game begins Repeatedly, this truth prevails.

What's more, in Ibsen's quote where he states, "the minority is rarely right" we find another truth about the markets. Yes, Columbus proved the world is not flat, and in the 1980s currency trader George Soros booked $1.1 billion—in a single day—by shorting the British pound, against the herd. However, those who triumph in the minority are a rarity. Usually, the minority is wrong, especially those who call for market crashes or for huge stock rallies based on expected earnings that are completely unrealistic. What all of this means is that we want to be part of the minority that is right—to take massive chunks of money out of the market—but we must continue to maintain a sense of reality and not let our own minority exuberance get the best of us.

The second quote by Ibsen reminds us that to truly make significant amounts of money in the markets, we must remember that at times we will need to find the strength to stand alone, something reiterated in the first quote, too. Superinvestors like Warren Buffett know this all too well.

In April 2008, Warren Buffett spoke to a group of business students at the Berkshire Hathaway headquarters in Omaha, Nebraska. *Fortune* magazine was on hand to record his words, quoting Buffett as saying:

"You know, I always say you should get greedy when others are fearful and fearful when others are greedy. But that's too much to expect. Of course, you shouldn't get greedy when others get greedy and fearful when others get fearful. At a minimum, try to stay away from that."[2]

Here is the crux: we must remember to buck herd mentality within the markets (at least when trading against the trend), while making sure to not to fall victim to exuberance when greed sets in. However, to do so, we must be strong enough to stand alone.

Case in point: In 2008, when the subprime debacle rattled U.S. housing markets, most investors ran from housing stocks like lemmings over a cliff. What's more, media headlines only helped to reiterate the fear by constantly pumping doom-and-gloom headlines about elevated foreclosure rates, housing prices falling through the floor, and the dismal future for homebuilders. The media did a good job of it, too, as most investors fearfully turned away from homebuilding stocks, assuming there was no hope. Funny thing, though, as Figure 1.1 shows, the U.S. Dow Jones Homebuilder's Index (DJUSHB) bottomed out in January 2008 and posted solid returns during the first quarter of the year, for those who bought housing stocks when the masses ran in fear. It's important to note the DJUSHB did fall to a new low in the summer of 2008, however, the index also remained reasonably resilient when the Dow fell through the floor in October of the same year. As of the time of this writing, the DJUSHB was still holding up from July lows, while the major indices had been crushed. As of the first week of October, the DJUSHB was down just over 9 percent for the year, while the Dow Jones Industrial Average had fallen over 27 percent. It's shocking to think housing was outperforming the broader market overall, something not many were aware of. (As this example shows, Warren Buffett's quote couldn't be any truer.)

Really, then, the second point of what investors need to know to make the most of this book is a point of common sense, though one that often bucks the intuition of the masses. No matter what any of the strategies

FIGURE 1.1 Dow Jones U.S. Homebuilder's Index (DJUSHB)
Source: Chart courtesy of StockCharts.com

within this book show you regarding a trade setup at any moment within the markets, it is vital for investors to remember to step back from the present state of affairs and consider the larger picture. A few savvy investors profited handsomely in homebuilding stocks during the first half of 2008 while the majority (fueled by media headlines) ran from housing like lemmings, but those savvy investors were only able to do so by stepping back from the situation, assessing the larger picture, and then having the mental fortitude to look beyond the problems at hand.

With all that you've just read in mind, please remember that if you take the time to remain objective, even while using any one of the strategies outlined in *The Swing Trader's Bible*, you stand the chance of seeing windfall profits in the years to come. Swing traders who had the insight to foresee the housing rebound of 2008 in December 2007, or even in January and February of 2008, could have used the LEAP covered call strategy outlined in Chapter 19 to protectively take positions in housing stocks. The point is that the strategies in this book are tools to help you successfully implement winning trades, based on both larger market ideas and micro technical occurrences. However, to be able to use these tools effectively, we must always step back from the masses and evaluate the bigger picture of every trade idea, headline, market paradigm, and even our own emotions. If we are able to do so, there is nothing stopping anyone at all from making all of their financial dreams come true.

Moving on, in Chapter 2, we will cover the first rule of profitability: stop loss, something that is vital for every trader to take the time to understand. By the end of Chapter 2, it will be clear that stop losses are more than just a way to contain losses. Rather, understanding how to use stop losses effectively is a tool that can increase your profitability over the long run.

CHAPTER 2

The First Rule of Profitability: Stop Loss

C onventionally, we think of stop loss orders as something rather simple, something to breeze over and then forget. However, as *The Swing Trader's Bible* shows, stops are actually incredibly powerful tools that increase profitability dramatically if used correctly. Really, stops are a trading tool, not just a simple way for traders to protect against losses. Fact is, when stops are incorporated as part of your trading strategy, you just might see your profitability greatly increase.

When most traders think about what causes them to initiate a trade, they think of items like fundamentals, technical signals, or news-related events. However, what traders should be thinking of is exit. Exit is everything.

The best traders in the world aren't those who can find great trades; rather, supertraders are those who know how to exit. When we think of the exit first, allowing the market take us out of trades, we remove emotion while also giving ourselves the highest potential to win, based on the simple fact that when we initiated the position, we predetermined our exit without letting our emotions get in our way.

THE END SHOULD ALWAYS COME FIRST

Take a moment to think about stop losses like driving. Do you ever get in your car with no idea where you're going? Sure, some may go for a Sunday drive on occasion just for the scenery or to get away and think, but arguably, most never just drive to drive.

Trading is the same: if you expect to get anywhere, you must have a destination in mind before you ever begin. Taking a position without a stop often results in getting nowhere at all, especially if trading conditions are choppy. The simple truth of the matter, though, is that most new traders never even consider where their trade is going, whether profitable or not. Most investors just take a position based on a great entry they think they see, without considering the potential outcomes. Please note that *outcomes* is plural, because every single time you buy or short a stock, one of two things is guaranteed to happen. You are either going to make or lose money. Period. Thus, investors who want to be successful must always consider *two* outcomes for every trade: how and where they will lock in profits, or where they will place the fire extinguisher that keeps the whole house from burning to the ground. This is going to sound a little rough: if you don't consider where you will exit a trade—should it fall to pieces—before you ever get in, you're kidding yourself, and eventually you're going to get smoked.

The previous statement is a cold, hard statement; however, a stock or option's trading range doesn't care one iota about you. And consider that whenever you place a trade, someone somewhere is on the opposite side, hoping to be able to take your money. Actually, they probably dream about taking your money, and if you leave your wallet just sitting on the table (taking a position without a stop), the second you're not looking, it will be gone. You can whine about it all you want, but it's your fault and your fault only for trading without the end in mind first.

Hopefully, you are significantly offended at this very moment. The discussion about stops is so *absolutely* important we have to beat this point home until investors see how absolutely irresponsible trading without stop loss orders is.

This chapter is brutal, isn't it? However, stay with us for a moment, and as you will see, the picture gets much, much brighter. Before we get to the good stuff, though, note that once in a while a devastating tornado will sweep the market, taking with it those who were unlucky enough to be in the way.

OCCASIONALLY UNFORESEEN DISASTER STRIKES

Take a look at Figure 2.1, and you will see a chart of Bear Stearns (NYSE: BSC), now owed by JP Morgan (NYSE: JPM). As you may already be aware, Bear Stearns fell through the floor in March 2008, when subprime losses extended into the billions. Ironically, Condé Nast, not generally known for

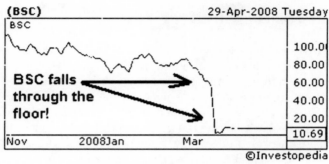

FIGURE 2.1 Chart of Subprime-Related Stock Slide of Bear Stearns in March 2008
Source: Reprinted with permission from Investopedia.com

its financial savvy, probably put it best when on March 14, its *Portfolio* magazine mused:[1]

> *What happened to Bear Stearns?*
> *It ran out of money.*
> *That can't be good if you're a bank.*

Humor aside, the situation isn't funny whatsoever. During the second week of March 2008, news began to trickle into the markets that Bear Stearns was experiencing liquidity difficulties because of losses in the mortgage markets. On Friday, March 14, the stock closed at $30 a share; however, when the opening bell rang on Wall Street the following Monday morning, the shares were trading at a meager $2 a share. Bear Stearns simply ran out of cash; thus, the Federal Reserve orchestrated a deal whereby JP Morgan would buy battered Bear Stearns for less than a cup of coffee per share.[2]

Investors who had stop orders outstanding took the same right hook on the chin as those who had no stop orders in place. Both sets of investors probably lost nearly everything.

The point here is that once in a while, bad things happen to good people, even in the market. Even stop loss orders won't save your money if unforeseen disaster strikes. However, the solution is simple: diversify. If you don't have all your eggs in one basket, they can't all get broken when an elephant escapes from the zoo on a mad rampage and stomps everything in its wake. At the end of the day, diversity is a stop loss tool, especially when it comes to your retirement portfolio, but that's another book in itself. We will now move into how stop losses are used as trading tools for profitability, first hard stops, followed by trailing stops, and finally, how to decide between the two stops in various trading scenarios.

HARD STOPS AS A PROFIT TOOL

Over the years, we've seen some of the best traders in the world blow up, only because they didn't have stops outstanding. Amazingly, even the most incredible traders in the world need hard stops outstanding.

Hard stops are more than just a place to protect our trades from falling through the floor. They are a tool that can help us consistently lock in profits, especially in volatile markets. Hard stops used with a few simple strategies can make a world of difference to the bottom line. Thus, we'll go over two hard stop strategies that can be used with trailing stops.

Hard Stops to Protect against Unforeseen Losses

When swing trading, we generally want to use hard stops on daily charts so as to not be wiggled out by intraday volatility. When you open a trade, you should always have a hard stop outstanding. It is vital to long-term profitability to always choose your first hard stop before you ever pull the trigger to buy or sell a market instrument. Why? Because when we determine our first stop loss point before we enter the trade, we are doing so from an unemotional standpoint. More often than not, when a trade begins to go against us, our emotions kick in, and—even for the best traders in the world—it's hard to think clearly when we're worried about losing money.

In using hard stops to protect against unforeseen losses, there are four stop rules to follow:

1. Always choose your initial stop point before you pull the trigger to buy or sell.
2. Immediately place a stop order after taking a position. Choosing a stop loss point but not placing an order is like riding a motorcycle with the helmet bungee-corded to the seat.
3. Determine ahead of time whether you will move your stop or (for shorter-term trades) have one only stop outstanding, after opening the position.
4. Always place stops on the opposite side of support/resistance and/or whole numbers.

The simple fact of the matter is, the longer you invest, the greater the chances that eventually you're going to place a trade that goes against you. It's how the bad trades are handled that separates the superstars from the hacks.

What's more, you may not always be at your computer. If a stock goes against you when you're not present, how will you ever protect yourself?

With this in mind, because we're swing trading—not position trading—we want to keep our stops as tight as possible while treading a very fine line of "not so tight" that we're stopped out of every trade. To clarify the fine line, we have to look at the larger picture behind the trade, so we understand where major technical support and resistance and trend lines are within our trade. Moreover, we also need to know where fundamental levels change. For example, as a stock ascends within a quarter, the trailing P/E ratio will grow, too. When the stock travels high enough, the P/E ratio could exceed the industry average and present a fundamentally overbought scenario. (We discuss ratios in greater detail in Chapter 3.)

Initial trade stops should always be placed on the opposite side of support/resistance and/or whole numbers. Figure 2.2 clarifies what we're talking about. Figure 2.2 is a *weekly* chart, not a daily chart. Sometimes, by using weekly charts instead of daily charts, we can cut the daily noise to see a stock's true trading range more clearly.

What we see is that that Exxon Mobil tested the $95 area three times in late 2007. Thus, resistance at $95 was clearly a strong valuation number, where funds and institutional investors were choosing to pass on the stock.

With that in mind, notice that contrarian traders probably shorted the stock in April 2008, as it once again neared the $95 area. The previous all-time high on the stock was $94.69, which, if investors had used it as a stop, would have forced the closure of positions. Exxon Mobil did breach December's high but failed to break above $95. Obviously, $95 serves

FIGURE 2.2 Weekly Chart of Exxon Mobil with Resistance
Source: Chart courtesy of StockCharts.com

as whole-number resistance. Thus, traders who put stops for their short positions—above $95—at perhaps $95.51, would have not been stopped out, even though the stock posted a new all-time high.

Hard Stops with Momentum

Now that we've covered hard stops to protect against initial losses, we can infer that if we're not stopped outright after taking a trade, then the trade must be working for us. One of the biggest mistakes of traders is letting a winner turn into a loser, which is an incredibly disheartening experience for almost anyone. Every trader eventually does it once or twice. Hopefully, though, if you haven't yet, by reading this chapter you won't have to experience the immense feeling of disappointment and stupidity when you let a winning trade leak into the red.

One of the easiest ways of using hard stops to maximize profitability is to simply ride the wave of momentum within your trade. This strategy is not only incredibly simple but also immensely effective.

In short, the hard stop momentum strategy is to continually ratchet up (for longs) or down (for shorts) your stop after the close of each trading day. Traders simply use the previous day's low, less a few cents (or a few dollars, if you're trading a really expensive stock like Google), as the stop point where you close your trade. When momentum is truly working in your favor, the stock, ETF, or index you are trading will continually put in higher lows successively (for longs) or lower highs successively (for shorts). Figure 2.3 shows exactly what we're talking about.

As you can see in Figure 2.3, assuming you had purchased the stock on trend line support, when the stock first started to take off, you would have wanted to immediately begin ratcheting up your stop. Then, the stock put in higher lows for 10 days. On the day 11, the long trade would have been stopped out for about a $10 profit. Not too bad, all things considered. However, if you notice, there was another break higher that could have given even more profits to those who were able to hold the trade.

To solve the problem of being unnecessarily stopped out, here are a few caveats, using the long trade in Figure 2.3 as an example. If we were trading short, all of the following information would be the inverse.

Use the daily low hard stop tool only when breakout momentum is significant. The Exxon Mobil chart doesn't really show huge momentum, but imagine successively larger breakout candles. Moreover, if the stock you are trading crosses over a whole number, use the whole number (placing the stop on the opposite side) as the stop until momentum begins to make your trade even more profitable. In the case of Exxon Mobil, by simply placing a hard stop at $79.49 after the stock crossed above $80, the trade would have capitalized on the second wave higher. Often when stocks cross above significant whole numbers, or resistance, they can

FIGURE 2.3 Weekly Chart of Exxon Mobil Higher Lows
Source: Chart courtesy of StockCharts.com

temporarily lose a little momentum as the market tries to make sense of the technical and fundamental events at hand.

When using momentum—and there is a *huge* breakout candle— perhaps parcel your position up into smaller parts (like 100, 200, or 500 share lots if you're trading 1,000 shares in each position), putting in stops at key Fibonacci retracements of the *breakout candle.* What we're doing here is giving the stock some room to wiggle after the breakout candle, without giving back *all* of our profits.

For example, you would put hard stops on 50 percent of your position at the 38.2 percent retracement, 25 percent of your position at the 50 percent retracement, and then the final 25 percent of your position at the 61.8 percent retracement. Notice we've closed half of the position at the highest retracement point, in relation to the breakout, so as to keep as much profit as possible.

USING TRAILING STOPS TO INCREASE PROFITABILITY

In today's world, chances are that you are pretty busy. If you're anything like us, you have 10 things happening at one time, both inside and outside the market. And for some of us, it's just too much to sit and watch our positions all day long.

You don't have to do that, though, at least not if you use trailing stops, which can help you capitalize on profits of intraday momentum without having to be there.

In a nutshell, a trailing stop is a stop loss order based on a certain percentage, or amount of points, in relation to the stock. Trailing stops follow the stock, as it moves, constantly adjusting as your trade becomes more and more profitable.

In essence, trailing stops allow you to lock in profits in a trade moving your way (both long and short), while also helping to minimize losses, should the stock suddenly bolt against you.

Imagine this scenario: You buy stock XYZ at $20 in a bold uptrend, and set your initial stop at $19. Over the following days, the stock ascends within just a few sessions, and your trade has gained $3.

At this point, you move your hard stop up to $22. You have effected a manual trailing stop by moving your stop up to protect your $2 in profits. However, you feel that on this particular day, the stock is going to have a massive breakout, after which the run could be over. What you could do is put in a 50-cent trailing stop, thus capitalizing on profit as the stock moves up. What's more, you are guaranteed $2.50 in profit, should the stock instantly crumble on the open.

The Risk: When effecting trailing stops, you risk being shaken (wiggled) out of your position if some sort of volatility ensues, whether stock-specific or market-specific. Also, trailing stops often require market orders, and if the stock begins to dump, the electronic order system might bring you a horrible fill. However, this is a risk with any type of market-related stop.

The Reward: At times, stocks can make dramatic upward movements (intraday) that you may not be at your computer to see. However, if a $20 stock were to jump $10 on a takeover rumor and then fall back through the floor that same day (rumors can often make a stock move erratically), chances are, your trailing stop would have given you $9.50 in profit. Trailing stops are great for making sure you capitalize on intraday moves but should probably not be used for longer-term trades, as in essence, they create a blind trading scenario, where we are not really in control of the situation. If volatility ensues, we could unnecessarily be stopped out of our trades. It's true that hard stops have the same issue, but the difference is that you are in control of hard stops, not the market and your computer.

At the end of the day, trailing stops are great candidates for momentum situations, where a stock is moving fast. By implementing a trailing stop, we are often able to exit at an ideal price when the momentum reverses, even when we're not at our computers. It's important to note that in illiquid stocks, we risk a poor fill if we are using a trailing stop with a market order. Thus, trailing stops are best reserved for highly liquid equities, where using a market order is not a concern.

Throughout Chapter 2, one point we hope to really bring home is that we should always have a distinct stop loss plan in place before we ever enter a trade. When we trade with the end in mind first, we remove ourselves from the momentary pressure that ensues if and when a position begins to move against us.

By using hard and trailing stops, we increase our profitability by protecting against losses. It's true we might take a hit once in a while if a stock completely falls out of bed; however, we could potentially take an even larger hit if we were recklessly trading without a stop whatsoever.

While some might prefer to throw caution to the wind and completely avoid stops altogether, eventually the chances are great a massive loss will ensue. The bottom line holds stops are really just good housekeeping, and the responsible way to trade. It's common sense really, which leads us into Chapter 3 on the very subject. What you're about to see is common sense, something so many investors and traders forget more often than not, truly rules the markets.

The Second Rule of Profitability: Commonsense Fundamentals

L et's get straight to the meat: studying fundamentals is often about as exciting as watching paint dry. At least, it seems that way at first, especially if you're not a weirdo Wall Street analyst. Really though, most analysts (usually) love what they do because they see that digging through numbers isn't a grind at all. At the end of the day, those numbers can mean big bucks.

However, the recommendations that most analysts compile are not what they put their actual money behind. Here's why: First, because of industry regulations, most of the time analysts can't buy the stocks they follow on record. Second, even when analysts dissect a company, most often they wouldn't have the faintest idea of how and where to find the perfect entry for a swing trade. Analysts are rarely traders.

We want to make you a sort of hybrid, though. We want to help make you an aggressive fundamental swing trader and technician. By doing so, you can find perfect technical entries for fundamental swing trades within stocks and options. Most short-term traders (swing traders and day traders) hardly ever imagine merging technicals with fundamentals, mostly because researching fundamentals seems like it would not only be complicated but also take forever. What we're going to show you here, though, is that you can easily gain a solid fundamental snapshot of a company in 10 minutes, or less. And as you're about to see, when you understand the underlying fundamentals of the trade, you're going to start finding profitable long and short opportunities all over the place.

We will use the term *technamental trading* to describe the merger of fundamentals and technicals. Following two brief notes, we will dive into the fundamentals behind technamental trading and investing. As traders and investors in the real world, we have developed these actual case studies to explain the fundamentals. This is not Wall Street, stuffy-suit theory; what you are about to read are the real, commonsense fundamentals used by real investors.

This chapter is one of the most important in the book, because what you are going to read here can be applied with every strategy in the entire book. The underlying fundamental picture within individual stocks *is* the core makeup of market movements.

Again, what follows are quick and dirty fundamentals applied and developed by traders, for traders. Elitist analysts may scoff at what you're about to read here; however, this commonsense approach does actually work.

CAREFUL WITH ETFs, INDEXES, AND OPTION VALUATION

This chapter is not meant to value indexes, or ETFs, other than comparisons like price to earnings (PE). The commonsense fundamentals within this chapter are meant to help determine whether a swing trade is fundamentally at hand, either long or short, within a company and the underlying stock or options.

In theory, you could tackle the fundamentals of all of the companies within an ETF, or index, but let's get real: you're probably not going to. However, the more investors begin to look at the common sense of fundamentals, the greater their chance of intuitively knowing whether the market as a whole, indexes, and/or ETFs are undervalued or overvalued. Investors who look at fundamentals—and who've been researching for years and years—just know, because they've seen the numbers of thousands of companies. In a moment, you will see what we mean.

One more note: This chapter does not apply whatsoever to option valuation. The option strategies at the end of the book will help you trade the underlying fundamental stock setup, but option valuation is another animal altogether.

COMMON SENSE IS KING

There is a fine line between winning because you know just enough more than the next person and knowing so much that you are wrong.

Here is what we mean: Warren Buffett, arguably one of the greatest investors in the world, routinely states that he invests only in businesses he understands. The skinny is that when we overcomplicate things to a point where it is hard to see the forest for the trees, we're usually worse off than when we started. Within short-term trading, we want to know what's going to move the market today, tomorrow, and a month from now. It does require looking ahead six or nine months sometimes, but when we overcomplicate the whole situation, we're going to be wrong because chances are, the other guys aren't going to understand the whole thing either.

We want to know what others know—or will see—and act accordingly. If we uncover something massive within an industry or stock that's pure genius, but is so complicated no one will ever be able to comprehend our discovery, obviously it won't matter in the short term.

What we're saying is, keep it simple and keep it real.

Here's a commonsense example: In 1999 and 2000, exuberance within telecom and fiber stocks was clearly abundant in the markets, as seen in many tech stocks hitting triple-digit price gains in a matter of months. Many analysts were chattering about the new valuation of technology that would derive grand, massive, blistering, *huge* revenue and net income from capacity and infrastructure. And then tech stocks tanked. Fact was, even with the "new economics" spouting in the media, the "growth premiums" placed within technology stocks at the turn of the century, defied common sense. One word to the wise, if you ever hear "new economics" in the market, whatever stock, or sector the term is applied to, is likely to get crushed. Fact is, business is business and income and revenue are the main drivers of business. When people say "new economics" they're usually attempting to help themselves believe more income and revenue will appear in the future, than common sense holds true. "New economics" usually means "go short."

Back to common sense analysis though, when it gets too complicated and the average Joe doesn't "get it", the situation probably defies common sense, and you should take a step back from your research to consider what's really going on under the surface.

With this in mind, we're now going to look at actual ratios that many have already seen over and over. However, by the end of the chapter, you will see how it pays to take another glance at commonsense fundamentals and ratios from the perspective of a trader.

RATIOS MATTER

One of the easiest ways to begin your commonsense valuation is to look at a stock's ratios, including price to earnings (PE), forward PE (FPE), price to earnings growth (PEG), price to book (P/B), and price to sales (P/S). However, these ratios mean nothing by themselves and always have to be taken into consideration with similar stocks and the individual company's next few quarters. Many think these ratios are "low brow"; however, for the common sense swing trader, "low brow" really means "clarity, simplicity and profit."

Trailing Price to Earnings (PE)

For the previous quarter, the ratio is derived by dividing the share price by earnings, otherwise known as an earnings multiple. It is often used to consider whether a stock's share price premium is fairly valued in regard to current earnings. The lower the multiple, the better (5 to 20), though a PE under five can be indicating that the market isn't pricing in much earnings prospect. You can do the actual math by dividing the current share price by diluted earnings per share (EPS). Using Yahoo Finance as an example, after you enter a stock symbol, simply click on the Key Statistics tab on the left-hand navigation bar to find diluted EPS (see Figure 3.1). On the lower left-hand side of the chart, you will see the actual diluted EPS number, which is 5.12 in the case of 3M. Then if we divide the share price (76.90) by diluted EPS (5.12), we get a trailing PE of 15. This number doesn't really mean anything to us yet; we must see the PE in the context of the larger sector.

By clicking on Competitors on the same left-hand navigation bar, we then see (though not shown here) the PE comparisons between 3M and three similar companies. What's more, we see the industry average PE, too, which serves as a benchmark for where the stock is trading, in regard to known earnings. In the case of 3M, the company had a PE of 15, and the industry average was the same. What this tells us is that for the most part, the stock is trading where it should be—at the present moment—with respect to the most recent four quarters of earnings.

What we are really looking for here is a PE that is significantly above or below the industry average, thus indicating that a fundamental swing trade might be looming (more on this in a moment).

Forward Price to Earnings (FPE)

Next on our list is basically the same ratio as the trailing PE, but the FPE takes into account estimates for the **next full year**, not the past four quarters or the current year. The FPE gives us an indication of where the stock is trading now, in relation to future earnings expectations.

What is important to know is this: because, in theory, earnings are expected to grow year after year if a company is healthy, the FPE should be lower than the trailing PE.

If the FPE is higher than the trailing PE, this should be an immediate red flag that future earnings are expected to decline. On Yahoo Finance, you can find both trailing and forward PE numbers on the Key Statistics

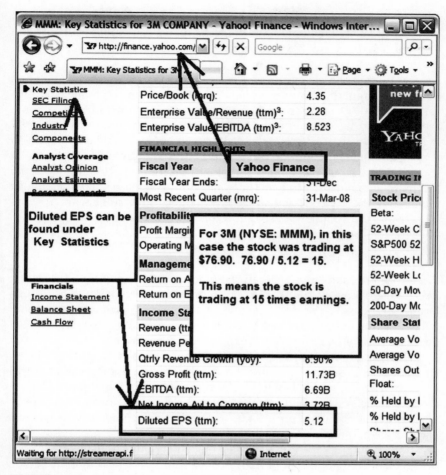

FIGURE 3.1 Key Statistics for 3M (NYSE: MMM)
Source: Yahoo.com

page, near the top left-hand side. Virtually every major **free** stock site (including MSN, SmartMoney, CBSMarketWatch, Morningstar, and Yahoo) already calculates the ratios in this section.

Price to Earnings Growth (PEG)

Price to earnings growth is similar to the FPE ratio, except that instead of dividing the share price by the following year's full-year EPS estimate, the share price is divided by earnings growth. As a general rule of thumb, when the PEG is near 1, the stock is generally considered undervalued. However, when the PEG nears 3, as a general rule the stock is beginning to look overbought in regard to future earnings growth. PEG can be found on most financial web sites, for example, under Key Statistics on Yahoo Finance. There are two caveats to PEG:

- PEG ratios can vary from source to source, as different data vendors use different time frames to calculate the growth rates. Some web sites calculate PEG on a three-year growth outlook; others use five years. However, five years of expected growth should be protocol. Yahoo Finance uses five years of expected data and thus is a reliable source.
- We previously mentioned that when a PEG approaches 3, the stock may be starting to become overvalued, but it is important to check the number against the industry average. Some industries like technology sometimes have higher average PEGs; thus, PEG numbers are only relative to the common sense of the sector average.

Price to Book (P/B)

Price to book takes into account the stock price divided by total assets, less intangible assets and liabilities. (Intangible assets include items like brands, franchises, patents, trademarks, intellectual property, and goodwill.) You don't need to calculate book value yourself, though, as virtually every major financial web site already does it for you.

What you do need to know is this: common sense tells us that when a stock begins showing double-digit book value, while the PE ratios and PEG are extremely high, you should be careful about buying the top.

Conversely, when book value falls to 1, or even below 1, the stock is probably undervalued in terms of the company's total assets on the balance sheet. Here is the caveat.

Book values at or below 1 indicate that something has happened within the stock or the sector that probably caused a massive sell-off in the stock. Often, the assets—in relation to the stock price—are undervalued. However, it is important to check to see why the book value is indeed so low.

In Chapter 1, you read: "Funny thing though, as Figure 1.1 shows, the U.S. Dow Jones Homebuilder's Index (DJUSHB) bottomed out in January 2008 and posted solid returns during the first half of the year, for those who bought housing stocks when the masses ran in fear."

Here we show you that chart again (Figure 3.2).

See, in January 2008, perceptive investors began to realize that homebuilders had been writing off inventory in previous quarters to protect against massive liabilities hanging out in the market with real estate crumbling on a national level.

Just after the turn of the year, many homebuilders were seeing P/B ratios right around 1.

FIGURE 3.2   2008 Dow Jones U.S. Homebuilder's Index Bottom (DJUSHB)
Source: Chart courtesy of StockCharts.com

The low P/B ratios told us that something was going on (which was obvious, as the subprime issues had made major headlines virtually every week over the past year).

Moreover, the low P/B ratios also indicated that housing companies were a good deal, based on balance sheet valuation alone. Smart investors noticed and probably profited on the bounce in homebuilding stocks throughout the first part of 2008. Really, it was common sense that housing markets in the United States would never completely implode and that the low P/B ratios were indicating the bulk of the damage was done. Simply put, on a commonsense level, when you can buy a stock close to the actual asset value, any future earnings growth is likely to translate into a premium in the share price.

Price to Sales (P/S)

Price to sales is one of our favorite ratio indicators as well, calculated by dividing the current share price by the revenue per share over the past 12 months. Many analysts overlook P/S, but traders should not. Here's why: price to sales does not account for expenses or debt; however, when price to sales falls far below 1, investors can infer that, fundamentally, business was much better in the past. What's more, should the underlying issues be repaired, the share price could easily rally significantly as the market perceives increased revenue translating to net income.

In the case of homebuilders, as we have already outlined, in the first part of 2008, many of the stocks were trading with P/S ratios from 0.2 to

0.8. These ratios were incredibly low and accurately reflected the fact that consumers had almost completely stopped buying houses. However, the low price to book ratios, too, indicated that homebuilders were also writing off inventory at the same time, as a proactive balance sheet strategy.

If price to sales is extremely low while price to book is—on a commonsense level—far too high, look out below, because 9 times out of 10, it means that exuberant investors are overpricing a company's assets, but trailing sales were not impressive.

With this in mind, we will now cover **what makes all of these ratios so powerful for swing traders** when used on a commonsense level.

EXUBERANCE IS NEVER FUNDAMENTAL COMMON SENSE

Here is a little secret about investing, (something that seems like it would be common sense but often is not): **Exuberant investors cannot see truth. They can only see what they are emotionally tied to**.

Many investors become emotionally attached to the stocks in their portfolios, which often means that they see only what they want to, even when news surfaces that opposes their opinion. The attempt at emotional detachment is exactly why—as swing traders—we focus on a small number of commonsense ratios, which all have to be used in unison not only looking at the company itself but also at the sector averages.

What's more, often investors who have purchased a stock do so because they have fallen in love with the story, over the fundamentals. They have found an incredible company that promises massive revenue in the future, because their products or services are *"just that revolutionary."* This is where common sense comes in. When we look at things like PEG, which shows price to expected five-year growth, and it is low, while PE, P/S, and P/B are all at reasonable levels, too, and the company's story has the possibility of mega revenue in the future, there might be reason to buy. However, when a company promises mega revenue but PE, FPE, PEG, P/S, and P/B are through the roof, common sense tells us, "Yeah, the company might have some amazing things cooking, but the future events are already priced into the stock now."

Exuberant investors just never get that last point. No matter how high (or low) a stock goes, they think it will just keep on going forever. Those investors—the exuberant ones—are the people who create bubbles in the market, based on unrealistic future expectations.

The simple, commonsense fundamentals in this chapter will be scoffed at by Wall Street analysts as not considering a variety of factors that contribute to value, or lack thereof. However, repeatedly, common sense through these simple ratios tells us whether a stock has upside left—on a simple fundamental level—or whether the top is near.

If someone pulled up in a shiny 2005 red Corvette that was beautiful on the outside but went clickety clack while exuding black smoke, and they told you that it has the possibility of running like a champ in the future so the price is $75,000, because when it's really firing on all cylinders, it would be worth $100,000, would you buy it? No way. Common sense tells us that a 2005 model certainly won't demand a collector's premium, and with the engine sounding like a can full of rocks, $75,000 would be ridiculous. The guy who's selling the Corvette probably really believes the car is worth that much, because he's fallen in love with it. Please, don't end up a victim of falling in love with a lemon with a shiny coat of paint on the outside. Really, anytime you fall in love with a stock at all, you should just get out, because when the tides turn, chances are you won't see the tsunami coming.

The ratios in this chapter are not just simple fundamental insights; they are commonsense guides to profitably trading stocks. On a commonsense level, using ratios within your trading can help you navigate stress when unforeseen market moves pull a trade in an unfavorable direction. By having some sense of the economics behind the trade, we not only become more cohesive investors on the whole but also are able to weather market storms with greater endurance.

Chapter 4 goes on to cover technical analysis and some basic charting techniques and technical indicators. Moreover, it discusses why technical analysis can be similar to a beacon in the night and how the concepts become self-fulfilling prophecies within the markets, especially in today's computer-oriented society.

The Third Rule of Profitability: Technical Analysis

T he third and final rule of profitability is technical analysis. All traders must have a strong grasp of reading the stock charts through technical analysis if they truly want to succeed at swing trading. The charts are the basis for several of the trading strategies introduced in later chapters. Many may find this chapter simple to grasp, but if you are struggling with the concepts, please do not move forward until you feel comfortable with all aspects of the chapter.

WHAT IS TECHNICAL ANALYSIS?

According to John Murphy, one of the greatest technicians in the stock market, technical analysis is the study of market action, usually with price charts, which includes volume and open interest patterns.[1]

We believe technical analysis is the study of past price patterns in the stock market based on supply and demand and trends. When analyzing a chart of a stock, an investor is looking at the past price movement of the stock. This movement was based on buying and selling of the shares, thus taking us back to the supply-and-demand theory. If there are more buyers than sellers, the price of the stock moves higher, as the market makers have to raise the price to make a market in the stock. The exact opposite happens on the other side, when there are more sellers than buyers; the price of the stock has to be adjusted lower.

I cannot tell you how many times I have been asked why a stock was higher on any given day. It could have been due to a good earnings report, a positive press release, or the approval of a new drug. The bottom line is that there were more buyers than sellers, and thus the stock closed higher for the day. Whatever the reason may be for the stock moving higher, it is reflected in the price of the stock, and this is why technical analysis will tell a story that fundamental analysis lacks—the truth.

This book will not go over all the detailed ins and outs of technical analysis, as we would likely never stop writing, and you'd get bored reading; there's just too much information to cover it all here. However, we will cover the basics quickly before moving on to how to use the charts to make money in swing trading.

THE BASIC CHART

The plotting of past prices is the most important aspect of a chart That is why we must look at the different types of charts available to traders. In Figure 4.1, there is a basic open, high, low, and close (OHLC) chart. Each bar tells the trader where the stock opened and closed and the high and low of the period. This is important because it gives details about how the stock acted throughout the chosen period. Figure 4.1 is a daily chart, and therefore each bar represents one full day of trading. Swing traders typically concentrate on daily charts but have also been known to use hourly charts or even shorter time frames.

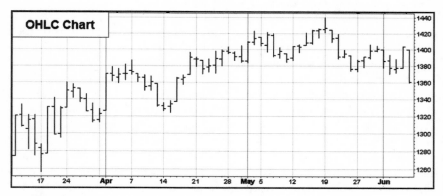

FIGURE 4.1   A Basic Open, High, Low, and Close Chart
Source: Chart courtesy of StockCharts.com

The Eastern version of the OHLC chart is Japanese candlesticks charts. The candlesticks also show the open, close, high, and low, but in a very different manner. The candlestick has two different parts, the body (shows the open and close) and the shadows (shows the high and low). In Figure 4.2, the candlestick chart shows the exact same information as Figure 4.1, but with a different type of chart setting.

The candlestick charts are covered in more detail in Chapter 12, but the basic fact you need to know is that they offer more visual insight into the action of the stock. Most successful technical analysts are considered visual beings, in that they can grasp a concept better with their eyes than with other senses. A candlestick chart offers more visual information from candlestick to candlestick than OHLC charts. There is no right or wrong choice when deciding which type of chart to implement in your trading strategy, but we will concentrate on the Japanese candlestick charts for the remainder of the book. Most traders use candlestick charts, thus, because we hope to capitalize on the "self fulfilling prophecy" aspect of technicals (meaning enough people are acting on the same information to make an expected event in the future come true), we will focus on candlesticks too.

Figures 4.1 and 4.2 showed the price movement of the stock only in a given time frame. In Figure 4.3, the Japanese candlestick chart is the same as Figure 4.2, except basic indicators have been added. The 50-day moving average is the line that is running through the candlesticks. Below the candlesticks is the volume indicator, and above is the relative strength index (RSI). Everyone will have a different basic chart they begin with, but this has been mine for the last several years.

FIGURE 4.2 Candlestick Chart
Source: Chart courtesy of StockCharts.com

FIGURE 4.3 Basic Chart with Indicators
Source: Chart courtesy of StockCharts.com

INTRODUCTION TO BASIC TECHNICAL ANALYSIS INDICATORS

Price Action/Trend

Price action is the most important aspect of technical analysis, and it is displayed in all charts, whether a line chart or a Japanese candlestick chart. I refer to the price action of the chart (also called the trend) as the backbone of technical analysis. The price is key because it tells traders where the stock has been, and based on that premise, technical analysis should help predict the future direction. And if you think about it logically, who really cares what the RSI or stochastic is doing? All we care about is the price action of the stock. Here's another way of thinking about it; descriptive statistics do a darn good job of using historical data to infer future trends. Well, price action on a chart is that historical data, just relayed on a visual basis, instead of in "standard deviations" and/or other statistical terms.

When it comes to price action, the trader must determine the trend of a stock, which is either up, down, or sideways (neutral). A majority of the time, a stock is in the neutral trend, basically suggesting the stock is trendless. Typically a trader will shy away from a stock that is trendless because the odds of choosing the direction of the next move are not truly in his/her favor. Laterally trading stocks are a gamble, unless another strategy like channel trading, or an options straddle are employed. However, when a stock is in the midst of a trend, the trader can either go with the trend or wait for a signal that the trend is ending and then go against the trend.

To determine the direction of the trend, a trader must analyze the peaks and troughs on the chart. An uptrend shows higher lows and higher highs; a downtrend is a series of lower highs and lower lows. In an uptrend, the trend line is drawn under the troughs and moves from left to right in an upward fashion. The downtrend line connects the lower highs and moves in a downward direction from left to right (see Figures 4.4 and 4.5).

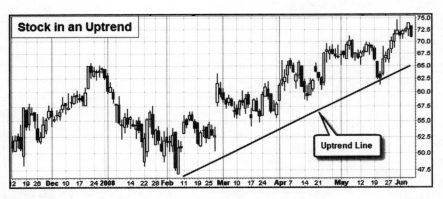

FIGURE 4.4 Example of a Stock in an Uptrend
Source: Chart courtesy of StockCharts.com

FIGURE 4.5 Example of a Stock in a Downtrend
Source: Chart courtesy of StockCharts.com

The length of the trend line is also important for traders. The longer the trend line, the stronger the trend; however, when a long trend is broken, the countertrend move is typically very violent. For example, when a stock makes a series of higher highs and higher lows for over a year, it displays the strength of the bulls. But when that strength begins to wane and the uptrend line is broken, the bears take over complete control, and the stock will fall hard. In Figure 4.6, the stock was in an uptrend for over a year, and when the uptrend was finally broken, it fell dramatically, offering a short opportunity for dexterous reversal traders.

There are four easy basic setups that traders need to know when it comes to the trend lines. They are illustrated in Table 4.1.

Support and Resistance

Support and resistance go together like peanut butter and jelly. Support can be defined as an area where buyers continually jump in and overtake the sellers, forcing the stock to rally. Resistance is the exact opposite,

FIGURE 4.6 Example of a Stock Breaking below the Uptrend
Source: Chart courtesy of StockCharts.com

TABLE 4.1 Playing the Trend	
Setup	**Trader's Action**
Stock pulls back to uptrend line	BUY
Stock breaks above the downtrend line	BUY
Stock bounces to downtrend line	SELL
Stock breaks below the uptrend line	SELL

an area where sellers continually jump into the market and push a stock lower.

Support and resistance can fall into a number of different categories, depending on how they are formed. Price resistance occurs when the stock regularly fails at a certain price level as the sellers take control. Price support takes place when a stock rallies from a price level as the buyers see a bargain at that price (see Figures 4.7 and 4.8).

The psychology behind resistance is that the bulls are taking their profits at prior highs and at the same time the bears are initiating short positions. The traders on the sidelines will play the short side of the resistance or, at a minimum, stay away from buying. The inequality of buyers and sellers results in the stock failing at the same price area as it has in the past.

FIGURE 4.7 Price Resistance
Source: Chart courtesy of StockCharts.com

FIGURE 4.8 Price Support
Source: Chart courtesy of StockCharts.com

The psychology behind support involves the bulls buying more of the stock when it pulls back to a price that has offered an attractive buying opportunity in the past. The bears will be exiting their short positions on the pullback, and the traders on the sidelines who have been waiting for an opportunity to buy will begin putting new money into the stock, thus creating a bottom.

Volume

If the price action is the driver of technical analysis, then volume is the fuel that powers the car. Of all the indicators, volume is the most reliable in determining the future movement of a stock. The reason is that all sustainable moves in a stock must have volume behind them or they will be short-lived.

First, let's define volume as the number of shares that trade hands in any given period of time. On a daily chart, the volume displays the number of shares that were traded during one full trading day. Volume can be plotted on all charts of all time frames, from a one-minute chart to a monthly chart.

When the volume is tied in with the trend of a stock, it gives more insight into the strength or weakness of the trend and which direction the stock is likely to move next. Table 4.2 is a reference table for traders who analyze volume and trend. When the volume is increasing, the trend has strength and will probably continue. When volume is decreasing, it suggests the trend could be coming to an end, and traders should look for a countertrend move.

In Figure 4.9, the chart shows volume decreasing as the stock comes to the end of the uptrend. This should have been the first sign to traders that the stock should not be bought and, even better yet, should be shorted.

In Figure 4.10, the chart shows volume increasing as the stock begins to rally in the early stages of an uptrend. The volume continued to flow into the stock for months, and alert traders would have had an inclination that this rally was coming when analyzing the volume.

TABLE 4.2   The Effect of Volume on a Trend

Price Trend	Volume	Stock
Higher	Increasing	Bullish
Higher	Decreasing	Bearish
Declining	Increasing	Bearish
Declining	Decreasing	Bullish

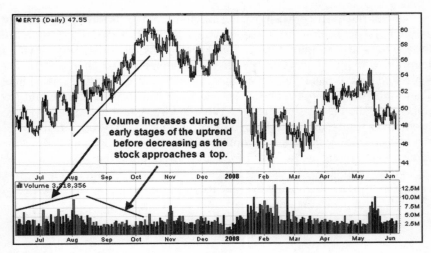

FIGURE 4.9 Decreasing Volume in Uptrend
Source: Chart courtesy of StockCharts.com

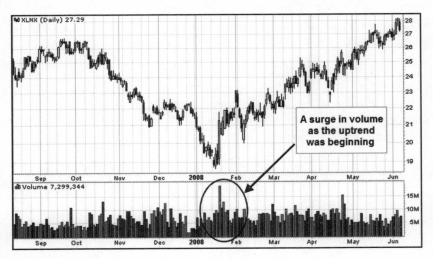

FIGURE 4.10 Increasing Volume in Uptrend
Source: Chart courtesy of StockCharts.com

Moving Averages

The most widely used indicator on the chart after volume would have to be moving averages. A moving average is a smoothing device that helps determine the trend of the stock. The moving average can be set for any time frame and can be used on all charts, regardless of the period they cover.

One of the most commonly used moving averages is the 50-day moving average. To determine the 50-day moving average, the closing prices of the last 50 days are summed together and divided by 50. This will give you a number, which is plotted on the chart. The numbers are then connected, which gives a flowing line that often acts as support and/or resistance. There are two types of moving averages that traders use, simple and exponential. The calculation just described is how a simple moving average is computed. An exponential moving average also uses the closing price of the last 50 trading days, but it weighs the more recent days more heavily. The simple moving average is more widely used, but the exponential moving average can give traders a better feel for short-term trading. Figure 4.11 compares the simple moving average to the exponential moving average to show the difference on a daily chart.

THE IMPORTANCE OF TECHNICAL ANALYSIS

Depending on whom you talk to in the investment industry, technical analysis is either voodoo or the best thing since sliced bread. I would have to fall in the middle and say technical analysis is essential for all trading systems and at the same time it is not the be all, end all. I have always found it hypocritical that the big firms shy away from technical analysis and concentrate solely on fundamental analysis for their clients, when in actuality every firm has a chief technical analyst who reads the charts on a daily basis. But then again, this should not surprise me because most of this

FIGURE 4.11 Simple versus Exponential Moving Averages
Source: Chart courtesy of StockCharts.com

industry is hypocritical, and that is why you need to learn to read the charts for yourself and use them in your swing trading strategy.

The most successful traders and investors implement a strategy that includes both technical and fundamental analysis, along with other secondary tools. The fundamental analysis is more important for long-term investors, and when it comes to swing trading, it can be ignored in certain situations. As you will see later, a number of trade setups are based solely on the charts and nothing more. When it comes to a four-day swing trade of a stock that is overbought, the revenue growth and P/E ratio of the stock are irrelevant. This is why it is imperative that all swing traders have a solid grasp of reading the charts.

A BEACON IN THE NIGHT: THE CHART IS YOUR FIRST ALERT

The reason technical analysis can be so very important to traders is that it can alert you to something going on with the stock before any news hits the wires. You may be asking how this is possible. Well, as much as everyone would like to believe that the stock market is efficient, it is not. Certain people are privileged to private information that can affect stock prices, and when they make their move, it is reflected in the charts.

Think about it. When was the last time you saw volume pick up three days before a stock is bought out for a 50 percent premium? Or how about big volume before a company releases an FDA approval for one of their drug candidates? Often volume spikes before a bullish earnings announcement; do you think all the buyers that pushed the stock higher before the positive announcement got lucky? Nope. Keep in mind this can happen on both big rallies and sell-offs. Look at Figure 4.12, and tell me that someone did not know there was going to be an announcement.

SELF-FULFILLING PROPHECY

The skeptics of technical analysis argue that past performance is no indication of how a stock will perform in the future. That is up for debate, and there are plenty of examples that will help me prove them wrong. But why does technical analysis work, and how?

Most technical analysts like myself will not admit to this, but I believe a large part of why reading the charts works is due to a self-fulfilling prophecy, that is, a prediction that becomes true as a consequence of having been made.

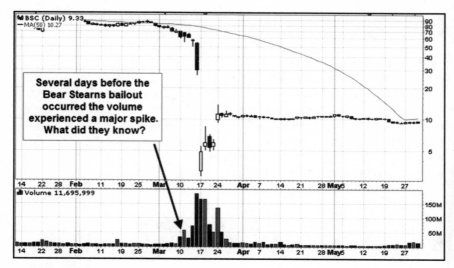

FIGURE 4.12 What Did They Know?
Source: Chart courtesy of StockCharts.com

FIGURE 4.13 Example of a Stock Bouncing off the 50-Day Moving Average
Source: Chart courtesy of StockCharts.com

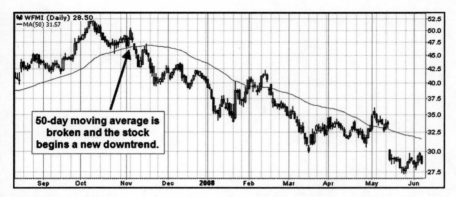

FIGURE 4.14   An Example of a Stock Breaking below the 50-Day Moving Average
Source: Chart courtesy of StockCharts.com

If most chart readers view the 50-day moving average as an important indicator, it will become an important indicator. When the S&P 500 pulls back to the 50-day moving average during an uptrend, the mass media will begin highlighting technical analysis and the support the indicator provides. If the 50-day moving average is held, it will lead to all the believers deciding that the moving average is a support level, and the buyers will overwhelm the sellers, forcing a rally in the stock market. On the flip side, when the 50-day moving average is broken on the downside during an uptrend, it will also make media headlines and send negative connotations throughout the market. Within days, you will see the S&P 500 fall, as the chart readers now believe the uptrend is over. Both situations can be seen in Figures 4.13 and 4.14.

CHAPTER 5

Strategy 1: Take the Trends to Pieces

I n Chapter 3, we showed how commonsense fundamental ratio analysis can give investors an incredible edge within the markets by being able to quickly determine whether a stock is nearing, or in, underbought or overbought territory. So say you put together some quick commonsense ratio analysis, and suddenly you realize that the stock you're looking at is rocketing through the roof, based on exuberance alone. You want to take a short position, but the question is where would be the lowest probability potential loss point to take that position, taking into consideration the fact that most investors have completely stopped looking at fundamentals anyway? The answer often lies within trend trading tools.

What's so amazing about trend trading tools, though, is even if a fundamental overbought or oversold situation isn't present, you can make it matter no matter what's happening—or at least as long as you have the ability to identify the trend at hand. Within this chapter, you're going to find two incredible tools to trade trends: channels/envelopes and pitchforks. Each allows you to find not only entry points for fundamental-based swing trades but also technical positions, even if there really isn't an apparent trend at hand anyway.

NOTE ON FUNDAMENTALS AND TREND TRADING

In Chapter 3, we covered commonsense fundamentals for swing traders. If you find a stock that on a commonsense level shows a fundamentally overvalued or undervalued situation, you can use the trend trading tools in this chapter to pinpoint your entry for the highest probability win potential.

The most profitable traders in the world are those who not only know how to identify great trades but also are patient enough for the market to come to them before they take positions. As an example, even if you find an overvalued stock, it may still have some upside left, as market exuberance takes it higher. Using trend analysis tools, you can identify a high-probability top, or target, where a low-risk short entry becomes available.

RIDING THE ENVELOPES

Envelopes are amazing when you see them traded correctly; there is no doubt about it. As you're about to see, for the swing trader, envelopes provide key short-entry buy and sell points.

Envelopes are often called moving average envelopes, and by definition, they are trading bands at a measured point, or percentage from a moving average. In other words, envelopes have three parts: a moving average, a top envelope (line), and a bottom envelope (line). The lines above the moving average are drawn based on a percentage off the moving average.

The actual math for the top band of an envelope:

Moving Average + (Moving Average + Percentage Offset)/100

The bottom envelope math:

Moving Average − (Moving Average + Percentage Offset)/100

The key to envelopes is figuring out what the volatility of the stock is, meaning the typical volatility a stock moves from the mean. Here's an analogy to clarify the reasoning of why envelopes often work in trading.

Imagine that your house is in the middle of the city, sitting right on the main boulevard that runs one mile south of your house and one mile north of your house. You know that when you're going shopping on the boulevard, you're probably going to walk one mile north, or south, as the bulk of the city's stores are on the boulevard. The farther you get to one end of the boulevard or the other, the higher the probability you will be returning to the center (where your house is—a metaphor for where the moving average is at any given point). The volatility is measured as a percentage of distance from your house, which in this case is one mile in either direction. The aforementioned is also known as "mean reversion."

With this in mind, the volatility of a stock's usual movement is the percentage, which will typically move above or below a moving average, before returning to the mean (moving average). While sometimes stocks move away from their moving averages, they *always* come back to the moving average, eventually—simply because moving averages move. One caveat to the previous statement is the number of days making up a moving average; the greater the probability the stock will not only travel farther away from the moving average, but stay away from the moving average—for a greater period of time—as well.

Using Exponential or Simple Moving Averages with Envelopes

When inquiring whether to use exponential moving averages (EMA) or simple moving averages (SMA) to trade envelopes, we must first ask in what time frame you are trading.

Shorter-term traders (day traders and swing traders seeking one- to three-day movements) will probably want to use exponential moving averages, as by definition, exponential moving averages are weighted giving more value to recent prices over a simple average of all historical prices.

Simple Moving Averages (SMA)   Simple moving averages are calculated by taking a set number of days, or periods, adding all of the values, and then dividing by the total. (A 5-SMA would be calculated by summing five days of closing prices and then dividing by 5.) The end value is a simple moving average of the last five closes. The SMA changes slightly each day, as the most recent day is added to the calculation, while the previous fifth day drops off, with the conclusion of each trading day.

Here's an example.

Day	Close Price	SMA
Day 1	$121.00	$121.00
Day 2	$122.00	$121.50
Day 3	$123.00	$122.00
Day 4	$122.00	$122.00
Day 5	$124.00	$122.40
Day 6	$127.00	$123.60
Day 7	$129.00	$125.00
Day 8	$125.00	$125.40
Day 9	$129.00	$126.80
Day 10	$133.00	$128.60

Exponential Moving Averages (EMA)   Exponential moving averages, on the other hand, using the five-day moving average would be calculated by first finding an exponent, which is the weighting factor behind the average. The calculation always begins by adding one period to the total period and then dividing by the constant 2.

The 200-EMA exponent (Exp) would be

$$5 + 1 = 6$$

Then,

$$\frac{2}{6} = 0.33$$

The actual formula calculating the EMA would then be

Close Price (CP) minus Previous EMA (PEMA) multiplied by Exponent (Exp) plus previous PEMA

which would look like:

$$((CP - PEMA) * Exp) + PEMA^{1}$$

Day	Close Price	SMA	EMA
Day 1	$121.00	$121.00	121.00
Day 2	$122.00	$121.33	121.33
Day 3	$123.00	$121.75	121.89
Day 4	$122.00	$121.80	121.93
Day 5	$124.00	$122.40	122.62
Day 6	$127.00	$123.60	124.08
Day 7	$129.00	$125.00	125.72
Day 8	$125.00	$125.40	125.48
Day 9	$129.00	$126.80	126.65
Day 10	$133.00	$128.60	128.77

As you will see in the daily data, the EMA generally stays closer to the actual close price of the stock, as more weight is given to the most recent period.

There are a couple of points that come out of this.

- Shorter-term envelopes should generally use EMAs over SMAs, as the exponential moving average more closely tracks the actual stock price.

- If you're looking at 50- or 200-day moving averages, so as to find a longer hold (and probably greater profit potential), SMAs are the moving averages of choice. Why? It comes down to market psychology. Fifty- and 200-day SMAs are the standard moving averages on virtually every chart on the Internet and within brokerage charting software. By using the 50- and 200-day SMAs over EMAs, we are exploiting the self-fulfilling prophecy of moving averages, based on larger market psychology.

Identifying Exuberance

Before we get into actually trading within envelopes, we need to cover one aspect of envelopes that must be covered: exuberance. Market or stock exuberance is when a stock is fiercely moving in one direction or another, based on market participants—basically—having lost their heads about the situation. Exuberance is usually the moment when we should stop and remind ourselves, "If it's too good to be true, it is probably isn't true." Exuberance ensues usually when good news within a stock, sector, or the economy drives investors to believe fortunes are easy to be made, or the sky is falling. The bottom line is, exuberance is a period when we generally do *not* trade in channels or envelopes and instead switch over to momentum strategies that focus on breakouts and breakdowns.

One simple trick with envelopes can help us identify exuberance. It's as easy as applying 50 percent envelopes to a 200-DMA. What you're about to see is pretty amazing. Looking at Figure 5.1 of Immersion Technologies (NASDAQ: IMMR), you will notice that in the spring 2007 the stock began to rip upward, after the company wrapped up a lawsuit with Sony (NYSE: SNE) and received a cash windfall. In June 2008, the stock pierced to the top envelope and was shortly followed by the 21-EMA.

Here's the rule: When a stock, index, or ETF pierces the upper or lower envelope (200/50 percent) and is followed by the 21-DMA, exuberance has set in, and we need to remind ourselves that momentum is clearly in play. What's more, we can profit from the momentum, so long as we refuse to let exuberance blinders keep us from understanding that a reversal is probably looming, and when it hits, it is going to hurt most people who do not have the capacity to invest with stops in place, or in other words, without common sense..

With Figure 5.1, there are five points to make, which we cover in just a moment. Importantly, though, by identifying exuberance, we can sometimes find great longer-term reversals that yield *massive* profits for patient

FIGURE 5.1 Immersion Technologies (Nasdaq: IMMR)
Source: Chart courtesy of StockCharts.com

traders. Thus, keep in mind, when exuberance sets in, the following points will prevail.

- Consider switching over to momentum strategies to trade with the trend.
- Look for a reversal entry, knowing exuberance will eventually end.

On the actual chart, there are five numbered points. Take a moment to look them over.

1. **Exuberance:** Here, we see where Immersion broke above the psychological resistance of the $10 whole number and began a torrid rally upward. Breakout/momentum traders probably did very well at this time.
2. **Confirmed:** When the 21-EMA crossed above the top envelope, the event would have been confirmation that exuberance was real, and breakout traders should begin using momentum strategies, if they had already not done so.
3. **First Shot Fired:** After rallying 100 percent, the stock quickly fell back into the top envelope in August. This was the first shot fired to

suggest that a reversal could be pending. After a large move, it is advisable to always wait for a double top before going short.

4. **The Final Blow:** Immersion tried to rally back above the top envelope, but this time, it quickly fell back below, with the coup de grace being that the 21-EMA could not make it above the top envelope.

5. **The Reversal:** Losing about 65 percent of the value from the stop in July, when the stock approached $7, reversal traders were probably chomping at the bit to buy the stock. Those who were patient enough to wait for confirmation that the stock would indeed not pierce the bottom envelope (confirmed when Immersion crossed back above the 21-EMA, which clearly stayed away from the bottom envelope) were up roughly 20 percent at the time we wrote this book.

What all of this indicates is that when we use envelopes with 200-SMAs and 21-EMAs, we are able to identify not only exuberance but also potential *huge* reversal winners as well.

Short-Term Channels/Envelopes

First and foremost, the number one rule of trading with short-term envelopes is that you absolutely must use them with common sense. Here's why: Unlike the 200-SMA envelope example, the volatility factor varies from stock to stock. Why? Because every stock is different in stability of income and revenue; economic, political, sector, and company news; and the investors who cover the sector. Common sense tells us that technology stocks are likely to be *more* volatile than waste management stocks. As a general rule of thumb, the more stable the revenue and net income, the less volatile the stock.

With this in mind, protocol for short-term envelopes is a 21-EMA, with envelope percentages usually around 5 to 15 percent, though the number can vary widely. In other words, on a short-term basis, stocks usually wiggle anywhere from 5 to 15 percent above and below the 21-EMA.

The entire point of short-term envelope trading is to attempt to capitalize on quick reversals, based on a stock moving to the upper and lower limits of the 21-EMA envelope. When the stock trades toward the top envelope, we want to short it, and when the stock trades to the bottom on the envelope, we want to go long. We also want to try to trade with the trend, if possible, to give the trade additional win probability of moving in the right direction, based on the larger trend. In sideways trends, short-term envelopes can easily yield swing trade profits both up and down.

The crux of trading envelope reversals is simply waiting until the stock pierces the upper or lower envelope and then comes off with confirmation.

We want to trade in the direction back to the moving average, using stops to protect out position (ratcheting the stop up or down, as noted in Chapter 2), as the stock moves in our favor.

Here's how it works: Using a 21-SMA, we want the stock to actually touch, or *pierce*, the upper or lower envelope and then confirm a reversal with an open **and close** (following the last day that pierced the envelope) off the envelope. The art behind envelope trading short-term movements is finding the magical envelope percentage that each stock is trading with at that particular time.

Looking at the chart of Exxon Mobil (NYSE: XOM) in Figure 5.2, we see a 21-EMA with 2 percent envelopes offset. You should immediately have a red flag in your mind, as obviously the 2 percent number is too small to give the stock the correct room to wiggle. Fact is, if you went short every time the stock touched the upper envelope at 5 percent, you would constantly get killed.

Now take a look at the chart in Figure 5.3 using 5 percent envelopes offset, and a whole different picture unfolds. (FYI: 5 percent is the general protocol for envelopes, though in many cases, the number can be much higher.)

What you will see is that over the past six months, every time the stock pierced the top, or lower band, and then opened and closed above or

FIGURE 5.2 Exxon Mobil (NYSE: XOM) with Envelopes
Source: Yahoo.com

FIGURE 5.3 Trades within Exxon Mobil (NYSE: XOM)
Source: Chart courtesy of StockCharts.com

below, respectively, the final envelope piercing candle, and using the final band-piercing high or low as the stop, six trading opportunities would have appeared, with five being big winners.

As you look at the chart, you will see the only loser was trade #2, where we entered short at roughly $91 and then were stopped out at $93. What's more, in trade #3, the stock declined from our entry, but after it touched the lower envelope, it opened and closed higher than the lower envelope—again—before taking out our initial stop in the $77 area, which would have prompted us to add to our position.

Overall, we needed some common sense to find the correct period where Exxon Mobil returns to the mean, after trading at the stock's upper and lower envelopes. However, by doing so, clearly five winners in six trades is an incredible swing-trading success. It's important to note that if we do not trade envelopes with solid money management (i.e., being able to follow our rules, without letting ourselves be scared out of a trade, ratcheting up stops, and then always taking profits when the stock hits the opposite envelope), we will lose. The simple fact of the matter is, to win when trading envelopes we must first use common sense, while also making sure we don't break our trading rules, especially if our emotions kick in with thoughts that vary from our original trading plan.

PROFITS THROUGH PITCHFORKS

Pitchforks, more commonly known as Andrew's pitchforks, are incredible trend-mapping and trading tools that can yield great profits for swing traders. It's important to note, right from the start, that a downfall of pitchforks is that they can fall apart in lateral markets. However, when a stock, index, sector, or ETF is displaying a clear trend, pitchforks can identify amazing entries, while also giving traders clear stop loss points to maximize risk management.

The crux behind pitchforks is this: a market instrument can often make a bold high or low, move out of the previous range, and create a short trough, or rally, which is the main identifier of the future trend to come. Because a picture tells a thousand words, see Figure 5.4.

This figure shows how a pitchfork is drawn on a chart. The starting point is the lowest low, just prior to the trough, which is the middle bar of the pitchfork. Investors simply dissect the trough at the exact middle and draw an extension line from the start through the trough midpoint, which creates the middle pitchfork. Then, simply draw parallel lines above and below the middle pitchfork, for the upper and lower pitchfork for the channel highs and lows.

Amazingly, pitchforks work over and over and over. Why? Conceptually, when a low is put in, followed by a move higher and then a decline

FIGURE 5.4 Pitchfork Setup with the Dow Jones Industrial Average (INDU)
Source: Chart courtesy of StockCharts.com

(trough), the trough basically sets volatility for the upcoming trend. What happens is more often than not, the market instrument will then trade within the channel or pitchfork until some type of market event occurs to change the course of events. So long as nothing major changes in the larger story, pitchfork channels generally stay intact. What's more, when a market instrument is trading on the lower pitchfork and begins a torrid rally, the middle pitchfork can be used as a profit target point, where a potential reversal could be looming. Pitchforks can be drawn both up and down on charts, as the overall concept is the same, regardless of direction.

Some call pitchforks median line studies; overall, though, they hold the same concept as envelopes in that we're simply using technical analysis to predict volatility in a trend. Pitchforks differ, however, in that during an ascending trend, when the lower pitchfork (ascending support) is violated with confirmation, the larger trend is usually ending, too. Conversely, in a descending pitchfork, when descending resistance is breached, a larger reversal is generally confirming as well.

In short, pitchforks are similar to envelopes as a guidance tool to volatility within a trend, allowing investors to buy and sell within the channel. However, envelopes do not indicate larger trend reversals, as pitchforks often show.

Now take a look at Figure 5.5, which shows how one could buy and sell within a pitchfork channel.

FIGURE 5.5 Pitchforks within the Dow Jones Industrial Average (INDU)
Source: Chart courtesy of StockCharts.com

As Figure 5.5 shows, once the pitchfork was established, traders would have had two opportunities to buy the Dow Jones Industrial Average. (The ETF DIAMONDS (AMEX: DIA) tracks the movement of the Dow, which investors can buy and sell, like a stock.) Both buy opportunities appeared on ascending support, the first in March 2008 and the second in April. In essence, channel trading through pitchforks is a way for investors to find low-risk entry points with clear stop loss points to take advantage of the short-term trend. What makes pitchforks ideal is the simple fact of clear stop loss points.

You will notice that the first buy opportunity appeared in March 2008 at roughly 11,800. The immediate stop would have been the low of the pitchfork, or roughly 11,700. However, the Dow held ascending support and immediately took off for the middle pitchfork, which is where investors would have wanted to take profits. Sometimes a market instrument trades all the way from the bottom pitchfork to the top pitchfork. However, it is recommended that investors take at least half of their profits off the table when the middle pitchfork is hit; usually when the middle pitchfork comes into play, consolidation ensues, before a continued move through the middle pitchfork. However, as the Dow chart shows, the index never traded through the middle pitchfork. Savvy traders who closed their trades the first time the Dow hit the middle pitchfork probably capitalized on an 800-point move in the Dow.

Next, the second buy opportunity appeared in April 2008 in the 12,200 area. Investors who purchased on ascending support would have used the late May low of 12,175 (approximately) for their stop. If the Dow had hit the late May low, ascending support would have been breached, and investors could then begin considering whether a larger reversal was occurring. However, the index immediately traded back above the 50-SMA and was again off to the races. At the time of this writing, the Dow was running into resistance at the 13,000 whole number, which would probably slow the Dow down some. However, the most likely outcome is that the Dow will make a spike higher to tag the middle pitchfork. Whether the Dow is able to hold ground or not depends on larger economic issues within the United States in 2008, however, with a reversal in the U.S. dollar looming against most currencies and the fact that it is a presidential election year, volatility will likely ensue. The mention of these nontechnical events is just a reminder that we have to look at what's happening within U.S. and global economies, along with the fundamentals behind individual stocks, to be the best traders we can be, even if we're trading with technicals.

Now that we've covered envelopes and pitchforks, we'll move on to relative strength in Chapter 6, something that will help swing traders capture momentum within individual stocks, while potentially saving a bundle when the walls begin to crumble.

Strategy 2: The RSI Indicator

T he relative strength index (RSI) is an overbought/oversold oscillator that is used to help identify peaks and troughs on a chart. The RSI was introduced to the trading world by J. Welles Wilder Jr. in his *New Concepts in Technical Trading Systems*. His indicator compares up periods versus down periods over a specified amount of time that the investor may choose. In the end, the RSI measures the strength of the stock versus itself. The exact formula is as follows.

RS = Average of x period's up closes/Average of x period's down closes

RSI = $100 - [100/(100 + RS)]$

The end result will be a number that ranges between 0 and 100. Readings between 70 and 100 are considered overbought, and readings between 0 and 30 are considered oversold.

Do not confuse the RSI with relative strength, another indicator that sounds very much the same. RSI compares a stock to itself, whereas relative strength compares a stock with an index or another stock.

CHOOSING AN RSI SETTING

The RSI calculation is based on the closing price on up periods and down periods. The period referred to in the calculation is most commonly one trading day. Traders who prefer to use 1-minute or 5-minute charts may use the RSI on their charts, and therefore each period would depend on the chart they are using. In this chapter, the RSI trading strategies are all based on a daily chart, and to make things less complicated, the word *day* will replace *period*.

The next step before finalizing the RSI calculation involves choosing the number of days that should be included. When Wilder developed the RSI, he recommended a 14-day setting, which takes into consideration the closing prices over the last 14 trading days. In reality, this is just short of three weeks of trading action. Some have said that a 22-day RSI is better for the long term, and others lean toward a 9-day RSI for trading purposes.

We use the nine-day RSI when analyzing the charts for potential swing trade candidates. Over years of using a variety of settings, we have found that the most accurate for the purpose of swing trading has been the nine-day RSI. This does not suggest you stop using your personal time frame for RSI. Keep in mind that there are a large number of indicators in the stock market and even more ways to implement them. They may not all work for everyone, but if it is working for you, do not stop!

The time frame you choose is important because it directly affects the amount of buy or sell signals that are generated. For example, in 2007 the 9-day RSI moved into overbought territory on the NASDAQ Composite a total of 8 times; the 22-day RSI ended with 0 appearances. As a matter of fact, the 22-day RSI did not once move above 70 or below 30 for the entire year. For a swing trader, that is not acceptable because 2007 was a very volatile year for the stock market, and moves into overbought and oversold territory are crucial to generating buy and sell signals.

RSI SWING TRADING STRATEGIES

There are several swing trading strategies in which the RSI is the primary indicator. The two strategies this book will concentrate on are the RSI crossover signal and the RSI divergence. The beauty of both strategies is that they are fairly easy to identify and can be programmed into most trading software to generate buy and sell signals automatically.

RSI Crossover Buy Signal

One of the most reliable buy signals for a high reward-to-risk swing trade is the RSI crossover buy signal (RSIX), which occurs when the RSI moves out of overbought territory (0 to 30) and back into the neutral zone (31 to 69). What makes this buy signal attractive to many beginning traders is that it is not subjective: either the RSI crosses above 30, or it does not. Of course, the crossover is not the only indicator a trader should be using, but it is a great start. (See Figure 6.1.)

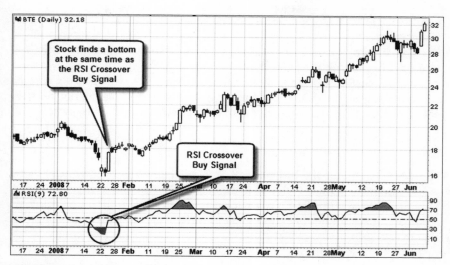

FIGURE 6.1 RSI Crossover Buy Signal
Source: Chart courtesy of StockCharts.com

The natural reaction from an inexperienced or unsuccessful trader is to buy a stock when the RSI moves into oversold territory from a neutral reading. The problem with this strategy is that a stock may be in the midst of a downtrend, and simply moving to oversold does not suggest the bottom has been formed. Buying a stock based on just an oversold RSI reading is no different from buying a stock hitting a new low. I like to refer to this type of strategy as trading suicide. Honestly, what are the odds that *you* pick the bottom and that the stock then moves higher from the time you buy? Not very good. Would you try to catch a falling knife?

Instead of trying to pick a bottom, we suggest you wait for a bottom formation to be built and look for the sweet spot of the pullback. Think of the sweet spot as the heart and soul of the rally. For example, the NASDAQ rally from 2331 to 2724 in mid-2007 lasted four months and consisted of nearly 400 points of gains. Realistically, an investor will not buy at the low and sell at the high. The sweet spot could be considered a purchase near 2400 and a sell in the 2700 area. The trader may get only 300 of the 400 points on the upside (or 75 percent of the move), but the risk is also much lower. Until a trader realizes that buying at the low and selling at the top is merely a dream, it will be difficult to make money on a consistent basis with any swing trading strategies in the stock market.

One word can sum up why traders must wait for the RSI to cross back above the 30 line: confirmation. When it comes to technical analysis, traders must understand that it is neither art nor science, but rather a combination of the two, that makes a successful technical analysis strategy. If it were 100 percent science, every time the RSI moved to oversold, it would indicate an oversold level, and a buying strategy would be the best option. Because technical analysis works the majority of time (if you have a proved strategy) but not all the time, traders must always wait for a confirmation signal. In the RSIX, the confirmation that a bottom has been formed and the stock is beginning to move higher is the move back above 30, out of oversold territory. This will capture the first half of the sought-after sweet spot.

RSI Crossover Sell Signal

What is great about the RSIX signal is that it can be used for both buying and selling. The RSIX sell signal occurs when the RSI line moves from overbought territory (70 to 100) back into the neutral zone (31 to 69). Just as a stock can continue to call in oversold territory, the same can happen on the upside. Often a strong stock moves higher for days, if not weeks, as the RSI stays in the overbought region. Trying to pick a top is often as hard as picking a bottom and can be even more dangerous when a momentum stock is rallying.

Staying with the momentum theme, the RSI can be a great tool to help a trader determine when a stock is running out of fuel near a top. If a trader is long in the stock, the RSIX sell signal can indicate when it is time to take the profit and sell. Or if the trader is attempting to go against the trend and prefers to play the pullback during an uptrend, the RSIX sell signal is the time to short the stock. An example of a momentum stock that was in the midst of an uptrend before pulling back is the Russian telecom company Vimpel Communications (VIP). In Figure 6.2, the stock hit a new high on December 10, 2007, and at the same time the RSI was also hitting a new high. The next new high that occurred during the last week of December was welcomed by traders who owned the stock. But the first sign of the stock getting overextended arose. The RSI made a lower high as the stock was making a higher high; this is referred to as an RSI divergence (we will cover this in a minute). Within two days, a RSIX sell signal occurred, and within three weeks, the stock fell nearly 30 percent from an all-time high.

If you were long VIP as a swing trade, the RSIX sell signal, coupled with the RSI divergence, would have been enough to force you to sell the stock. Investors who were looking to play the sell-off could have benefited from the RSIX by shorting the stock on the sell trigger.

Increasing the Odds of the RSI Crossover Signals   No buy or sell signal is perfect; therefore, traders should always be looking to improve their odds when entering or exiting a position. One simple way to do this is by going with setups that have more than one associated buy or sell signal. The VIP example has two sell signals, but both are related to the RSI.

FIGURE 6.2 RSI Crossover Sell Signal: VIP
Source: Chart courtesy of StockCharts.com

Preferably the RSIX signal would be combined with a different indicator, such as a moving average or trend line. The more signals that are in your favor, the better the reward-to-risk setup becomes, and your odds of entering a winning swing trade improve.

In Figure 6.3, FTI Consulting (FCN) was trending sideways for a few months, in the midst of retesting support at $26, and at the same time sitting on the 200-day moving average. A few days after holding the low from December and the moving average, the stock began to move higher as an RSIX buy signal occurred. The combination of the RSIX, bouncing off the 200-day moving average, and double bottom increased the odds of FCN moving higher in the coming days. Within a few weeks, the stock was higher by 30 percent.

The RSI Divergence

What makes the RSI divergence strategy so popular among traders is that it is often a precursor to a top or bottom. It often signals the end of a trend and can be a savior for traders who are in a position too long.

The RSI divergence occurs when the stock is making a new high or low and the corresponding RSI is failing to do the same. For example, in

FIGURE 6.3 RSI Crossover with Accompanying Indicators: FCN
Source: Chart courtesy of StockCharts.com

Figure 6.2, the Russian telecom company Vimpel Communications is making a new high and at the same time the RSI is failing to hit a new high. This indicates a loss of momentum in VIP that is brought on by internal weakening. Even though the stock may be hitting new historic highs, the strength at which it is rallying is diminishing, and traders should begin to consider selling their shares or, at a minimum, placing tight stop loss orders. Thus the bearish RSI divergence is formed.

The bullish RSI divergence is the exact opposite and can be used by traders who are attempting to buy a stock that is pulling back from a high or that could be hitting a bottom and preparing to reverse a downtrend. (See Figure 6.4.) In either case, the trader should have another indicator backing up the divergence before considering a buy order. The best indicator in this situation is price itself; if the price of the stock begins to either form a consolidation pattern or rally off the lows, the probabilities increase greatly.

IMPLEMENTING THE RSI STRATEGIES STEP BY STEP

To help you better understand the RSI crossover signal, we will highlight a stock that generates a signal and take you step by step through the swing trade process.

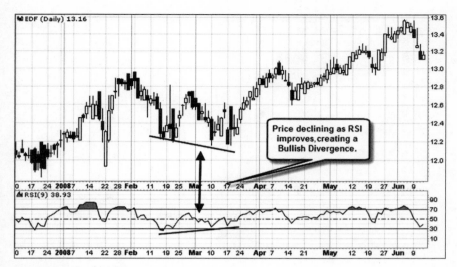

FIGURE 6.4 Bullish RSI Divergence
Source: Chart courtesy of StockCharts.com

In Figure 6.5, EnCana (ECA), an energy stock, generates an RSI crossover buy signal in late January 2008. At the time, the stock was in the midst of a pullback, but the candlesticks were beginning to improve, with the stock closing above the opening price for three consecutive days. On the day the RSI buy signal was triggered, the stock hit a new multi-month low before rallying to close up for the day. The combination of the RSI crossover buy signal and the bullish action of the candlesticks was enough to register a swing trading buy opportunity. The stock closed that day (1/23/08) at $61.00. Over the next nine days, the stock got as high as $68.97, a gain of 13 percent. Most swing traders would have locked in profits before the high and been happy with a quick gain.

Figure 6.6 shows that ECA continued to rally until mid-March, when an RSI crossover sell signal was generated. The chart also shows that the RSI buy signal on January 23, 2008, turned out to be the low of the year so far for ECA.

BRINGING IT ALL TOGETHER

One of the advantages of the RSI indicator is that it can be used in several different manners to generate both buy and sell signals. Once the RSI has been added to the trader's repertoire of trading tools, it will increase

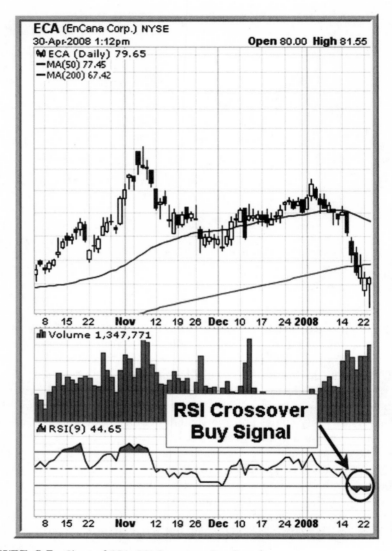

FIGURE 6.5 Chart of ECA: RSI Crossover Buy Signal
Source: Chart courtesy of StockCharts.com

the winning percentage dramatically. As much as I may believe in these RSI strategies, traders must remember that it still remains a secondary indicator. An RSI buy signal alone is not sufficient to warrant an order to purchase shares. The price action and trend must confirm the signal, thus increasing the odds of the trade being profitable.

FIGURE 6.6 Chart of ECA: Result of the RSI Signal
Source: Chart courtesy of StockCharts.com

Traders must also remember that the RSI is just one of the over-bought/oversold oscillators available in technical analysis. Its close cousins are the MACD and stochastic, discussed in great detail in the next chapter. The benefit of understanding all three indicators will become evident when all three generate the same buy or sell signal. This situation does not happen very often, but when it does, you will be able to take advantage of the high-probability setup. After you finish Chapter 7, you will know exactly what I am referring to.

Strategy 3: MACD and Stochastic

T wo of the more common and useful trading indicators are the MACD and stochastic. When the two are combined, they can make a powerful tandem that will improve your swing trading bottom line. The goal of strategy 3 is to introduce you to two more indicators that most traders are already using. When the masses are using an indicator as a sign for support and resistance, it often works because it is simply a self-fulfilling prophecy. That being said, this chapter offers with both indicators a variety of strategies that may not be the norm.

By the time you thoroughly read this chapter and begin putting the strategies to work in your real-life swing trading, you will understand how important both MACD and stochastic are to your trading future. Keep in mind that neither indicator is the holy grail, but comprehending both will improve your trading skills.

UNDERSTANDING MACD

The MACD acronym stands for Moving Average Convergence Divergence indicator. It is considered an oscillator and is used by both traders and investors. The MACD is most often used to help spot overbought and oversold levels of a stock. To construct the MACD, there must be two moving averages, the long and the short. When the indicator was originally developed by Gerald Appel, the two moving averages used were the 12-day and 26-day exponentials. There is also a third moving average, considered the smoothing portion of the indicator, which is necessary to the equation. The 9-day exponential moving average of the MACD is plotted on top of the MACD.

To calculate the MACD, the longer moving average (in this case, the 26-day exponential moving average) is subtracted from the shorter moving average (12-day exponential moving average). The line is placed on a scale against the 9-day exponential moving average of the MACD. The end result is a series of two lines that oscillate around the number zero. The buy and sell signals are generated a number of ways that are discussed in this chapter.

Before jumping into the strategies of how a swing trader can use the MACD, we explain the indicator in more detail to help you understand why the crossovers and divergences are so important.

In Figure 7.1, the daily chart of Johnson & Johnson shows the 12-day exponential moving average and the 26-day exponential moving average. There are traders who simply use the two moving averages and look for crossovers to signal buy and sell swing trade opportunities. When the shorter moving average crosses above the longer moving average, it is a buy signal. During the third week of March, the shorter moving average crossed above the longer moving average, giving a buy signal. When the two moving averages are equal to each other, just before the crossover, the MACD line will be at zero because the calculation subtracts the 26-day

FIGURE 7.1 Moving Averages That Make Up the MACD Indicator
Source: Chart courtesy of StockCharts.com

from the 12-day. If the two moving averages are equal, the resulting line to be plotted on the MACD would be zero.

If you do not fully understand where the MACD calculation comes from, that's okay. By the end of the chapter, you should understand and be on to the money-making part.

SWING TRADING STRATEGIES USING THE MACD

The most widely used strategy implemented with the MACD indicator involves identifying crossovers between the MACD line and the signal line. The second strategy is the divergence between the action on the MACD and the price of the underlying stock. The third strategy uses the MACD as an overbought/oversold gauge; when the indicator is at the extremes, it can keep swing traders from making hasty decisions.

Trading MACD Crossovers

The most reliable and easiest way to use the MACD is to look for crossovers, which occur when the MACD line (also referred to as the *fast line*) crosses above and below the signal line (also referred to as the *slow line*). When the fast line crosses above the slow line, it generates a buy signal. When the fast line crosses below the slow line, a signal to sell or go short is triggered.

In Figure 7.2, which is a daily chart of crude oil, you will see numerous buy and sell signals over a six-month period. The three buy signals have been highlighted with arrows that point to the corresponding price on the chart. The first buy signal did not catch the bottom, but the price of oil did move another 5 percent after the MACD crossover buy signal. In December, the buy signal was very close to picking the bottom of the short-term pullback, and the price of oil rallied over 10 percent during the next two weeks. The third and final buy signal occurred in February and was one day late on picking the bottom. In the month after the MACD crossover buy signal, the price of oil rose over 25 percent.

The same daily chart of crude oil generated three MACD crossover sell signals. Figure 7.3 highlights the three sell signals with arrows. The first MACD crossover sell signal occurs in November and gives the trader only one day to profit from a short sell. The second sell signal occurs in January and catches half of a sell-off that could have generated a profit of 8 percent for the short seller. The third sell signal in March called the short-term top in oil, only to see the price spike back up one week later. A nimble

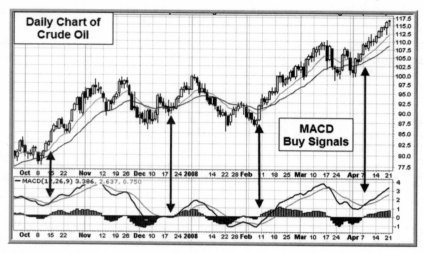

FIGURE 7.2 MACD Crossover Buy Signals
Source: Chart courtesy of StockCharts.com

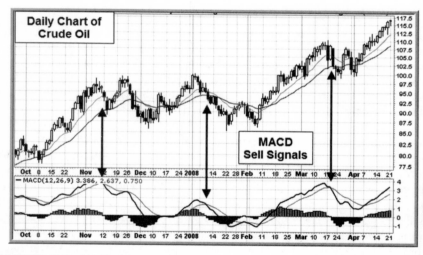

FIGURE 7.3 MACD Crossover Sell Signals
Source: Chart courtesy of StockCharts.com

swing trader had the opportunity to make a quick 5 percent profit on the downside.

As you can see, the MACD crossover buy signals were more profitable for swing traders and offered better reward-to-risk setups. The number one reason for this difference is the long-term trend of the chart. The price of oil has been in an uptrend for several years, and therefore shorting the chart of oil is a countertrend trade and not as favorable as going with the long-term trend. That is why it is critical for a trader to first determine the long-term trend, also known as the path of least resistance, before initiating a swing trade. Do not get me wrong. There is money to be made on countertrend moves. But if you would like to increase your odds, go with the trend and stick to the MACD crossover buy signals when a stock is in an uptrend.

There is one issue that many swing traders despise about the MACD crossover setup, and that is false signals. Just like any swing trading strategy, there is no perfect indicator that always generates winners. There are two ways that swing traders can use to eliminate false signals and become better traders.

The first step is to look back on the chart to determine if the MACD crossover signals worked in the past. If they worked 80 percent of the time, I suggest using the current signal. On the other hand, if the crossover signals generate winning trades only 50 percent of the time, then it is not worth your time and money to trade the stock. When the odds come down to a coin flip, it is time for you to move on to the next trade.

The second step a swing trader could take involves not relying solely on the MACD indicator, or any one indicator by itself. Often the RSI or stochastic gives signals at the same time as the MACD; the more indicators giving you a similar signal, the better your odds of picking a winner. There is also price action that must be analyzed before entering any trade. If the stock generates an MACD crossover buy signal and at the same time is bouncing off price support or an important moving average, the odds increase in your favor. As you will notice throughout the book, more factors in your favor result in more profitable trades.

The daily chart of Cal-Maine Foods in Figure 7.4 is an example of an MACD crossover buy signal coinciding with the stock bouncing off price support and forming a bullish double bottom pattern. The buy signal resulted in a big rally in the coming weeks that turned into a new uptrend. What makes the Cal-Maine trade so attractive is the high reward-to-risk setup. The reward is a rally from $22 to the most recent high of $31.46, and the risk is approximately $1. That is a 9-to-1 setup that no swing trader can turn down.

Trading MACD Divergences

An MACD divergence occurs when the trend of the MACD line and the price action begin to go in different directions. In essence, a divergence occurs when the stock is hitting a new high and the MACD fails to do so. A divergence can also occur when a stock is hitting a new low and the MACD

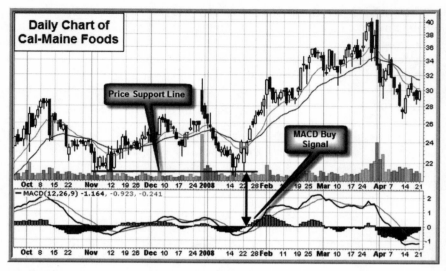

FIGURE 7.4 MACD Coinciding with Support
Source: Chart courtesy of StockCharts.com

is not making a new low. In Alexander Elder's "Trading for a Living," he refers to price divergence as "the strongest signal in technical analysis." I have great respect for Elder and agree that price divergence is one of the more reliable trading signals available.

In Figure 7.5, Costco Wholesale was in the midst of an uptrend in November when the MACD began to diverge and move lower. In early December, the stock rallied to a new high, and at the same time the MACD failed to hit a new high, thus giving traders an MACD divergence sell signal. The sell signal proved to be correct, and the stock was on the verge of a two-month downtrend that saw the stock fall nearly 20 percent. Note that the MACD gave a crossover sell signal a few days after the divergence. As I alluded to earlier, the more signals in your favor, the more likely the trade is to be profitable.

The MACD divergence does not always signal the exact top or bottom, but what it does well is signal a potential change in a trend. This is helpful to the trader in two ways. First, it helps you determine when it is time to short a stock that is losing steam or buy a stock that is oversold and due for a rally. Second, and possibly more important, the divergence keeps you out of potentially dangerous trades.

A swing trader may look at the Costco Wholesale chart in Figure 7.6 and consider buying the stock a couple of days after the breakout to a new high. This would have been a losing trade that could have been avoided by

FIGURE 7.5 MACD Bearish Divergence
Source: Chart courtesy of StockCharts.com

FIGURE 7.6 MACD Bullish Divergence
Source: Chart courtesy of StockCharts.com

noticing that the MACD was diverging from the price action. Swing traders must remember that not every stock is a buy or a sell; as a matter of fact, most stocks are no trades that should be avoided at all costs. The indicators we cover in this book generate buy and sell signals and at the same time eliminate poor trades.

The MACD divergence also works well when you are attempting to buy a stock that is preparing to bounce off the lows. In Figure 7.6, the Gardner Denver chart, the stock hits a new low in January after it breaks through the November low. The MACD is not moving with the stock and has been strengthening during the selling. When the new low is hit in January, the MACD is not hitting a low, and one day later an MACD crossover buy signal is generated. In the next two months, the stock rallied $10 and broke the intermediate-term downtrend.

Even though Alexander Elder considers the price divergence to be a great technical analysis tool, keep in mind that all indicators have their pros and cons. The MACD divergence signal can be very reliable when used properly, but the one problem that I have with trading it is that often it requires the trader to go against the trend. For example, the Gardner Denver chart would require a swing trader to buy a stock at or near a new low in anticipation of a rally. In my years of trading, I have found that traders who continually attempt to pick bottoms and tops end up picking themselves up off the floor after the market beats them down. In other words, it is not the best long-term strategy for becoming a profitable swing trader.

Trading MACD Overbought/Oversold Levels

The MACD is a mix between an oscillator and a momentum indicator. The momentum aspect is highlighted in the crossover trading strategy, and the oscillator part is used in finding overbought and oversold levels. The more extreme the levels of the MACD, either high or low readings, the more they become significant for swing traders. Remember, the middle line on the MACD is the zero line (when the long and short moving averages are equal). When the number gets too high, it suggests the stock is overbought and due for a pullback, and vice versa.

Because the MACD is constructed using the 12-day and 26-day moving averages, when the number increases, it represents the 12-day moving average at a higher level than the 26-day moving average. When the shorter moving average is well above the longer moving average, it typically implies the stock has recently made a big run higher and is due for a pullback. In Figure 7.7, the chart of Flowserve highlights an MACD that was extremely overbought and marked a short-term top; a 10 percent drop in price followed the overbought reading. The main reason the overbought readings work well at picking tops and bottoms is because it is not natural for the two moving averages to be very far apart. When the distance increases, it suggests extreme levels on the upside or downside, and the stock typically moves back to the norm and in the opposite direction of the recent move.

FIGURE 7.7 MACD Overbought Sell Signal
Source: Chart courtesy of StockCharts.com

When trading on the overbought and oversold levels, a trader should never base a decision purely on the MACD reading. For starters, the MACD may be overbought at a reading of 4.0 but move to 6.0 before the stock starts to fall. In many instances, a stock can continue to rally in overbought conditions or drop to new lows when extremely oversold. The best way to use the overbought/oversold readings on the MACD is in conjunction with other oscillators and with price action. Adding the RSI indicator to the MACD helps you determine the validity of the reading before moving on to price action. This does require another step in the stock analysis, but becoming a successful swing trader requires time and effort.

There will be other unique ways to use the MACD in trading that you will come across in your readings. Stick to the basics, and do not over-think the trading process. The only other strategy you should consider is using the zero line as a buy and sell signal. When the MACD line crosses above the zero line, it generates a buy signal, and crossing below the zero line results in a sell signal. However, we do not feel it is one of the better swing trading strategies available.

Now that you have a solid understanding of the MACD, it is time to introduce the next indicator, the stochastic. The two are related because they find stocks that are preparing to bounce after a pullback or that are near the end of the current uptrend. When the two are used together, they create a more reliable buy/sell signal.

STOCHASTIC

The stochastic indicator was invented by George Lane in the late 1950s and has since been a favorite of short-term traders. The theory behind the indicator assumes that a price increases and closes near its highs during an upward-trending pattern. When a stock is in a downtrend, the indicator assumes the stock will be closing near the lows of the trend. To come up with the numbers needed for the indicator, the closing prices during the period chosen are analyzed, and two lines are formed.

The formula looks like this:

$$\%K = 100[(C - L14)/(H14 - L14)]$$

where

C = the most recent closing price
L14 = the low of the 14-period trading range
H14 = the high of the same 14-period trading range

As you can see in the formula, the number 14 has been chosen to construct the %K line. The most commonly used period is 14; this can be applied to a daily chart, a weekly chart, or even an hourly chart. The smaller the number, the more signals occur, and vice versa. We have found the 14-day stochastic works well for identifying swing trades. The formula helps to determine the relationship of the most recent closing price to the range of the 14-day span.

The second line needed for the indicator is the %D line. This is simply the three-period moving average of the %K line. The two lines are then plotted on the chart and always fall between 0 and 100. Similar to the RSI indicator, when the stochastic is above 80, it is considered overbought, and below 20 is an oversold reading.

Fast Stochastic versus Slow Stochastic

To make things even more confusing, traders have modified the stochastic indicator to include a fast version and a slow version. In the fast stochastic indicator, the preceding formula is used, and the %K line is plotted along with the %D line. Remember that the %D line is simply a three-period moving average of the %K line and is referred to as the signal line. The problems traders have with the fast stochastic are the number of buy and sell signals. Because there are too many signals being triggered, the reliability of the indicator is low. To combat this issue, traders decided to smooth the line even more.

In the slow stochastic, the %D line, which is the three-period moving average of the %K line, becomes the %K line. The new %D line is the three-period moving average of the new %K line, thus creating lines that are much smoother than the fast stochastic indicator. There are fewer buy and sell signals when the slow stochastic is used, and therefore some traders see the slow stochastic as the more reliable indicator. In Figure 7.8, the chart of Bucyrus shows the difference between fast and slow stochastic indicators. By comparing the two indicators, it is obvious that the slow stochastic is much smoother. In January, the fast stochastic gave two false buy signals before the third signal marked the bottom. The slow stochastic gave only one buy signal, which coincided with the third signal on the fast stochastic. In the end, the decision to go with the slow versus fast stochastic comes down to personal preference. From our experiences, it is our decision to use the slow stochastic because of its reliability for swing trading.

Summary of the Stochastic Lines

%K (Fast) = the number generated from the preceding formula

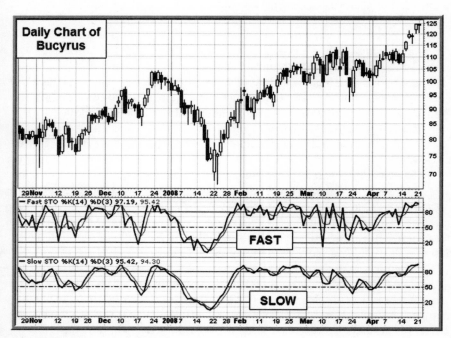

FIGURE 7.8 Stochastic (Fast versus Slow)
Source: Chart courtesy of StockCharts.com

%D (Fast) = three-period moving average of %K

%K (Slow) = three-period moving average of %K (same as %D fast line)

%D (Slow) = three-period moving average of %K slow line

HOW TO TRADE THE STOCHASTIC

For the remainder of the chapter, when we refer to stochastic, we mean the slow stochastic indicator. The stochastic can be used by swing traders in the same three manners as the MACD indicator: divergence, crossovers, and overbought/oversold levels.

The most widely used strategy with the stochastic indicator is spotting divergences between price action and the action of the stochastic. For example, when the price of a stock is hitting a new high and the stochastic is trending lower, it is a signal that momentum is waning and that a top could be near. The same type of strategy can be used for a buy signal. When the price of the stock continues to hit new lows, but at the same time the stochastic is strengthening, a buy signal occurs, suggesting the stock is near the end of the downtrend.

In Figure 7.9, the chart of Mechel Steel Group shows the stock hitting a new high in late December, but at the same time the stochastic was weakening. The higher high during the last week of the month was accompanied by a lower high on the stochastic. There are two ways in which the swing trader can play the divergence. The first is shorting or selling the stock when the stock hit the higher high and the stochastic failed to join the breakout party. This strategy often produces an early entry that can be very lucrative and, at the same time, dangerous because the signal may be too early.

The second strategy is waiting for the stochastic to cross out of overbought territory (above 80). This crossover strategy works very well with the RSI indicator and is one of our favorites with the stochastic. There are fewer buy and sell signals because the confirmation of the crossover is needed, but in the end it results in a higher percentage of winning swing trades, which is our goal with this book.

The crossover strategy uses the two lines, %K and %D, as the trade triggers. When the %K crosses the %D, it triggers a buy or sell signal, depending on the direction of the crossover. When the %K crosses up through the %D, a buy signal is generated. When the %K crosses below the %D, a sell signal is generated. The crossovers may occur anywhere on the chart, but we focus only on crossovers that occur in overbought (above 80) or oversold (below 20) areas. When a crossover buy signal occurs in oversold territory,

FIGURE 7.9 Stochastic Divergence
Source: Chart courtesy of StockCharts.com

it alerts traders to a potential buying opportunity. Traders are given a sell signal when the crossover occurs in overbought territory.

In Figure 7.10, the chart of Intuitive Surgical has two distinct bullish stochastic crossovers in November and March. In each situation, the arrows point out that the stock bottomed and rallied for the next two weeks. In the future, I now know that the likelihood of Intuitive Surgical rallying after a bullish stochastic crossover is high; therefore, I put the stock on the watchlist, and the next time the crossover occurs, I will buy shares of the stock.

The third and final trading strategy for the stochastic indicator entails looking at the chart and determining if the stochastic is overbought or oversold. When the stochastic is between 20 and 80, it is useless for this strategy.

There are two ways to use the overbought/oversold strategy. The first involves selling or territory. I would never recommend using this as the only indicator and basing a buy or sell simply on overbought or oversold. It is very common to see a stock that continues to rally for weeks in overbought territory. I consider using this portion of the strategy only if the price action gives a buy or sell signal and the stochastic confirms the original trade idea. For example, in Figure 7.11, the chart of Tesoro shows the stock failing at a double-top pattern, and at the same time the stochastic is overbought. A couple of days later, the sell signal is confirmed when the

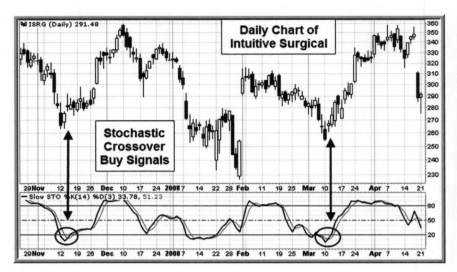

FIGURE 7.10 Stochastic Crossover Buy Signal
Source: Chart courtesy of StockCharts.com

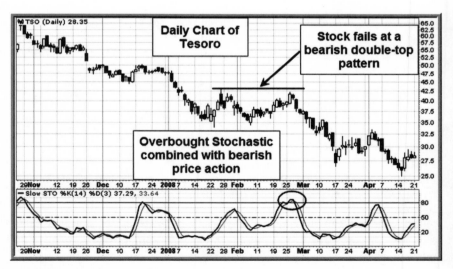

FIGURE 7.11 Overbought Stochastic with Bearish Price Action
Source: Chart courtesy of StockCharts.com

%K line crosses below the %D line and the 80 level, two high-probability sell signals.

In a second way, swing traders can use the overbought/oversold levels to their favor. Sitting in overbought territory is not a sell signal by itself. However, when the stochastic leaves overbought territory, it now becomes a sell signal worthy of swing trader's consideration. The same can be said on the flip side; when the stochastic leaves oversold territory, it is a buy signal. As always, when more than one indicator confirms the signal, your chance of entering a winning trade increases dramatically.

To recap, three trading strategies can be used along with the stochastic indicator. The first involves divergences that occur when the stochastic and the price are not moving in unison. The second is crossovers, which occur when the %K line crosses the %D line. The third trading strategy involves identifying overbought and oversold levels on the stochastic indicator. All three have their benefits, and all three have their flaws; in the end, you are likely to discover one or two that you feel comfortable with and concentrate solely on them.

CHAPTER 8

Strategy 4: The Tier II Play

FOLLOW THE LEADER

T he stock market is somewhat like a group of ducklings following their mother. Often, the little guys follow the big ones. In essence, tier II stocks generally follow tier I stocks. Another way of saying tier II plays is sympathy plays. See, when a stock with a massive market cap, or one that is simply a leader in the industry, experiences an event triggering a large rally, or a massive breakdown, Wall Street infers the smaller stocks are likely to experience the same, or perhaps even more so, given most smaller businesses' inability to pad themselves like larger conglomerates. Really, what it all comes down to is a swing trading strategy based on following the leader.

Amazingly, when a market leader makes a significant move, it would seem logical that the smaller—highly correlated—stocks would probably move at the same time. However, as unintuitive as it seems, this is not the case. Sometimes it can take days, even weeks, for news to move through an entire sector, once an initial breakout or breakdown appears. It's not that the rest of the sector (and the sympathy plays) isn't aware of the leader's breakout or breakdown, or that the news hasn't made it through to investors. The reason for the lag is the simple fact that Wall Street can be slow to act, even when acting quickly would be in the best interest of most holding the stock. However, the "hope factor" is what causes tier II plays from immediately reacting. The hope factor holds that many who are holding a highly correlated stock, to one that has just been completely crushed, "hope" it won't happen to their holding. But when it does, the panic begins.

To reiterate, the "hope factor" is nowhere more apparent than in breakdowns within a sector. If a large stock reports some sort of news that creates a massive landslide, it would seem that smaller stocks would suddenly make the same move, too. However, many investors generally won't sell right away, hoping that the news that took the big stock down will not affect the smaller company they invested in. Moreover, it can take a few days for the news to truly sink in and force many (even fund managers) to face reality. When the selling begins, though, it comes fast—something you are going to know how to take advantage of, after reading this chapter.

First, you need to understand what makes up Tier I, II, and III stocks. There is no set definition for the tiers, but as a general rule of thumb, the larger a company or the greater the market swagger, the more likely the stock is to be a tier I company. We'll detail here what actually makes up tier I, II, and III stocks; however, some common sense is required, as unfortunately, there just isn't any real one-size-fits-all model for determining tier status.

MARKET CAP IN TIERS

Market cap is the primary method of determining what tier a stock is in. Usually, the larger the market cap, the closer to tier I the stock is. Generally, we're talking about large, medium, small, and micro caps. The market cap is *not* a steadfast rule, specifically placing a given stock in a particular tier. It is a rough guideline that requires some intuition. At times, a small or medium cap stock can actually take on tier I status, something shown later in the chapter. For now, though, use this outline.

Tier I	Large and Mega Cap Stocks
Tier II	Medium Cap Stocks
Tier III	Small and Micro Cap Stocks

Again, note that market cap is not always the final determination of a stock's tier; rather, it's a primary filter to make the decision. In addition, when discussing tiers, investors must understand that the concept is both organic and dynamic. By this I mean that a stock's tier status is something more or less determined by market actions, income and balance sheets, and other current events.

Here's an example. Long ago, just after the turn of the century, Corning (NYSE: GLW)—we called the stock Glass on the trading floor—was a leader in fiber optic technology. And in the dot.bomb heyday, the stock's price reflected such, trading at better than $100 per share.

When Glass moved, many of the other fiber stocks (and semiconductors) moved as well. However, when the market began falling through the floor in late 2000, fiber stocks were some of the first to get beaten down. (See Figure 8.1.) (The entire Global Crossing debacle helped fuel the massive sell-off within fiber stocks, too!) Wall Street had priced in expected capacity and perceived future revenue the companies would earn, not only thinking that fiber would soon reach a point where it would be squeezed for capacity but also inferring that demand would soar. Nevertheless, when the dot.bomb ensued, many Internet and technology companies began going out of business, and the fiber companies were left with excess capacity, which the market quickly took as a major sell signal. At the end of the day, investors were expecting fiber companies to see windfall profits, and when business began slowing, the same fickle investors who drove fiber stocks through the roof dumped them just as quickly. In a matter of months, fiber stocks were no longer leading other tech stocks; many had—almost overnight—gone from expensive, triple-digit share prices to penny stocks. Investors who were still looking to fiber stocks for Tier I plays probably found themselves scratching their heads when trading strategies that had previously worked suddenly didn't anymore.

What all of this comes down to is the simple fact that we must use common sense when trading and understand that larger shifts in the economy and market can quickly chop the feet out from under Tier I stocks. To maximize Tier II trading, as well as investing overall, we must always remain clear-headed when a paradigm shift is underway. In short, we must be perceptive enough to recognize the moments when the big picture is changing.

At the end of the day, though, when a stock's price begins to decline, so does the market cap, as the two go hand in hand. Should a stock fall from grace, perhaps from large cap or medium cap status to small cap stature,

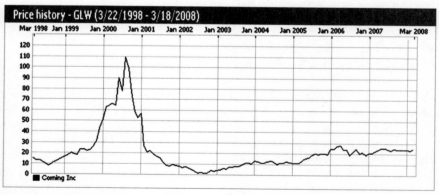

FIGURE 8.1 Corning Price History
Source: Chart courtesy of StockCharts.com

the likelihood of the stock continuing to lead other stocks within the sector (that are still performing) wanes as well.

Here's an example of a tier II stock in regard to the sector leader and an actual trading scenario where investors could have made money with this strategy.

EXAMPLE IN ACTION

Surely you are aware of the subprime debacle that hit America hard in 2008. Truly, I think we are all pretty tired of reading about it. However, within the whole mess were some of the greatest tier II and III setups I have ever seen.

As of March 2008, subprime losses were topping $175 billion, with analysts expecting the number to reach the $600 billion area when the dust settles. As news and estimates of billions in losses began to surface, bombshells began exploding within the market. One of the major hits was directly on Bear Stearns, which lost more than $20 billion in market cap from January to March 2008.

Fact of the matter is, was, and will be that the subprime news hurt virtually every broker and banker within the market. Nevertheless, when the Bear Stearns news broke, and JP Morgan agreed to buy the investment banking house for $2 a share, the bulk of the sector tanked, too. Figure 8.2 shows the 2008 returns for brokerage stocks, as of March 2008. In addition, it is here that the story gets interesting.

The primary determination of tier II stocks to their tier I counterparts is the correlation coefficient, which is a descriptive statistics tool that helps us determine how similar two stocks are. Generally, when two stocks have similar business models (regardless of market cap), their stock prices are likely to trade similarly.

WHAT TO LOOK OUT FOR: HIDDEN CORRELATIONS

Here's an example: Exxon Mobil (NYSE: XOM) and Chevron (NYSE: CVX) are both major oil and gas companies with similar business models. Although some of the fundamentals within the companies differ, the overall revenue and income models are relatively the same. The correlation for the two stocks is 89.2, which is extremely high and confirms that the two companies are very much alike.

Sometimes, though, a few companies have virtually no apparent correlation but move in sympathy with another company in an industry that, at first, seems unrelated. Take eBay, for example. As you are probably aware,

Symbol	Company Name	Last	Avg Vol	YTD Percent	52 Week High	52 Week Low
ETFC	E*TRADE FINL CO	3.61	34593524	1.69%	25.79	2.08
LTS	LADENBURG THALM	2.05	271655	-3.30%	3.18	1.49
NMR	NOMURA HOLDINGS	15.24	558430	-9.01%	22.08	13.08
MER	ML CO CMN STK	46.63	31134990	-13.13%	95	37.25
JMP	JMP GROUP INC	7.29	91260	-14.03%	13.2	5.62
AMTD	TD AMERITRADE H	16.52	5094185	-17.65%	21.31	13.82
AMPL	AMPAL-AMER ISRA	6.06	46555	-18.00%	8.5	4.27
GS	GOLDMAN SACHS G	175.59	16933530	-18.35%	250.7	140.27
MS	MORGAN STANLEY	42.86	20012780	-19.30%	90.95	33.56
KBW	KBW INC	20.27	611570	-20.79%	37.44	18
IBKR	INTERACTIVE BRO	25.59	1494220	-20.82%	35.93	20.25
MKTX	MARKETAXESS HOL	10.15	155290	-20.89%	19.87	8.83
SEIC	SEI INVESTMENTS	25.27	1092715	-21.45%	33.12	22.45
SCHW	CHARLES SCHWAB	19.25	16751980	-24.66%	25.72	17.41
COWN	COWEN GROUP INC	6.99	171820	-26.50%	19.91	6.29
LEH	LEHMAN BROS HLD	46.49	41375516	-28.96%	82.05	20.25
FCSX	FCSTONE GROUP I	31	1005285	-32.65%	53.25	18.17
TRAD	TRADESTATION GR	9.36	704760	-34.13%	14.87	8.43
OXPS	OPTIONSXPRESS H	20.57	1402830	-39.18%	34.95	18.55
TWPG	THOMAS WEISEL P	7.76	232575	-43.48%	21.05	7.18
MF	MF GLOBAL	8.17	8919265	-74.04%	32.2	3.64
BSC	BEAR STEARNS CO	5.91	39383836	-93.30%	159.36	2.84

FIGURE 8.2 2008 Performance of Brokerage Stocks
Source: Chart courtesy of StockCharts.com

eBay is the world's largest online auction house. However, a correlation study on eBay found that the closest counterpart is Cintas (according to Market Topology), which is basically a uniform manufacturer. Obviously, the two aren't similar at all.

However, when there is an online company sell-off, eBay usually shows some sort of price movement. When companies like Google suffer, eBay generally shows similar price action, at least in the short term. Thus, we have to remember that at times, some companies can be caught in larger moves of companies that aren't exactly even in the same sector.

WHERE TO FIND TIER II PLAYS

First, when looking for tier II plays, all you need to do is find a stock that has presented a major move within the market. For example, during earnings, stocks can make major moves based on either exceeding or disappointing Wall Street or by raising or lowering future guidance.

Usually, any of these changes result in a larger move within the underlying stock, especially in the case of a major breakdown within the company.

Here's why the tier II play works so well. Often, it can take the market a few days to digest earnings information, not only for the company that reported results but for the broader sector as well. And where there's smoke, there's fire, to put it bluntly. More often than not, if one company reports horrid earnings, the other companies within the sector are facing similar difficulties as well, unless the problem is individual to the company in question. If investors begin to realize that the issues are not just company-specific but are due to larger issues within the industry or the economy, tier II and highly correlated stocks will fall in following days.

Here's an example: In the early part of 2008, subprime woes had already rattled real estate markets, but the evidence was only starting to show up in other areas of the market, like building supply companies. During the week of February 25, both Home Depot and Lowe's reported earnings, first Lowe's and then Home Depot. Both sets of earnings reports stank. Here's the first paragraph of the press release from Home Depot, highlighting just how bad the situation was.

Tuesday February 26, 6:00 am ET

ATLANTA, Feb. 26 /PRNewswire-FirstCall/—The Home Depot®, the world's largest home improvement retailer, today reported fiscal 2007 fourth quarter consolidated net earnings of $671 million, or $0.40 per diluted share, compared with $925 million, or $0.46 per diluted share, in the same period in fiscal 2006. Sales for the fourth quarter totaled $17.7 billion, a 1.5 percent increase from the fourth quarter of fiscal 2006. [1]

By Thursday of that week, the market began to realize that building supply stocks were definitely in the wrong place at the wrong time, and the stocks began to fall out of bed, or at least Home Depot and Lowe's did. As the market is slow to react, though, Building Materials Group—not a brand name most people know—held ground, barely falling at all. Then, on the last day of the month, Home Depot gapped down, while Building Materials Group actually gapped up (Figure 8.3).

Most people would think that Building Materials Group would move with Home Depot, but the reality of the situation is that often the market is slow to price in news and events. On the last day of February, investors

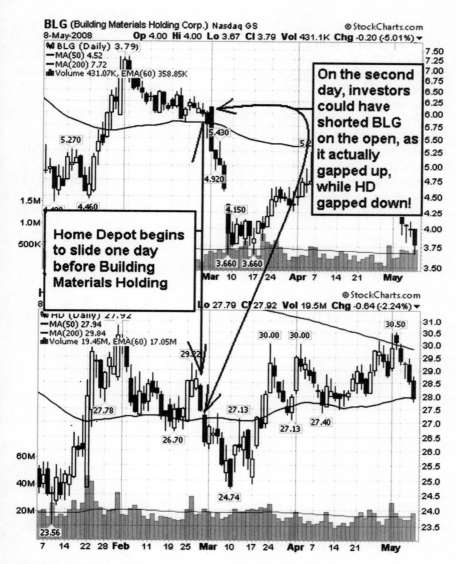

FIGURE 8.3   Home Depot and Building Materials Group
Source: Chart courtesy of StockCharts.com

could have shorted Building Materials Group, as it gapped up while Home Depot gapped down, and then seen a quick windfall in the subsequent days.

Hopefully, you can see how slow the market is to react sometimes. When a tier I stock makes a major move, quickly find other highly correlated stocks within the sector—ones that have yet to move—and you might just see some *huge* winners!

When using the tier strategies, remember that common sense is required because there really isn't a specific law for identifying what a stock's tier is. However, when you simply watch the trading action, it usually fairly easy to identify which stocks are leading and which are not. Once you've identified several sets of tiers, you can simply sit back and wait for one of the leaders to move and then seek a position in a laggard. Really, what it all comes down to is that stocks (investors, actually) are pack animals at heart.

CHAPTER 9

Strategy 5: ETF Sector Rotation

N early everything that occurs in this world or in life can be connected to a cycle. According to www.dictionary.com, a *cycle* is "any complete round or series of occurrences that repeats or is repeated." *The American Heritage Dictionary* gives a slightly different view: "An interval of time during which a characteristic, often regularly repeated event or sequence of events occurs." Both definitions include the word *repeated*, which is very important. In a cycle if an event is repeated, we should be able to anticipate when the event will occur again.

In the stock market, there are a number of different cycles that can produce profit if we have an idea of when the event will repeat. Of course, there is no guarantee that the cycle will continue or that it will repeat in the order anticipated. However, learning the different market cycles adds another tool to make you that much better of a trader in the future.

ASSET CLASS MONEY ROTATION

You will be hard-pressed to find a long period when one of the major asset classes was able to outperform its peers. Figure 9.1 shows the returns of the major asset classes from 1987 through 2006, ranked from best to worst each year. The first asset class that jumps out of the chart is the S&P/Citi 500 Growth stocks. From 1995 through 1998, the group was the best performer, putting together the longest such streak in the 20-year period. The strong performance lasted one more year before the asset class moved to

Reproduced From the Callan Periodic Table of Investment Returns

Annual Returns from key Indices (1995-2007) ranked Order of Performance

1995	1996	1997	1998	1999	2000	2001	2002	2003	2004	2005	2006	2007
S&P/Citi 500 Growth 38.13%	S&P/Citi 500 Growth 23.97%	S&P/Citi 500 Growth 36.52%	S&P/Citi 500 Growth 42.16%	Russell 2000 Growth 43.09%	Russell 2000 Value 22.83%	Russell 2000 Value 14.02%	LB Agg 10.26%	Russell 2000 Growth 48.54%	Russell 2000 Value 22.25%	MSCI EAFE 13.54%	MSCI EAFE 26.34%	MSCI EAFE 11.17%
S&P 500 37.58%	S&P 500 22.96%	S&P 500 33.36%	S&P 500 28.58%	S&P/Citi 500 Growth 28.25%	LB Agg 11.63%	LB Agg 8.43%	Russell 2000 Value −11.43%	Russell 2000 47.25%	MSCI EAFE 20.25%	S&P/Citi 500 Value 4.91%	Russell 2000 Value 23.48%	S&P/Citi 500 Growth 9.13%
S&P/Citi 500 Value 36.99%	S&P/Citi 500 Value 22.00%	Russell 2000 Value 31.78%	MSCI EAFE 20.00%	MSCI EAFE 26.96%	S&P/Citi 500 Value 6.08%	Russell 2000 2.49%	MSCI EAFE −15.94%	Russell 2000 Value 46.03%	Russell 2000 18.33%	S&P 500 4.91%	S&P/Citi 500 Value 20.81%	Russell 2000 Growth 7.05%
Russell 2000 Growth 31.04%	Russell 2000 Value 21.37%	S&P/Citi 500 Value 29.98%	S&P/Citi 500 Value 14.69%	Russell 2000 21.26%	Russell 2000 −3.02%	Russell 2000 Growth −9.23%	Russell 2000 −20.48%	MSCI EAFE 38.59%	S&P/Citi 500 Value 15.71%	Russell 2000 Value 4.71%	Russell 2000 18.37%	LB Agg 6.97%
Russell 2000 28.44%	Russell 2000 16.53%	Russell 2000 22.38%	LB Agg 8.70%	S&P 500 21.04%	S&P 500 −9.11%	S&P/Citi 500 Value −11.71%	S&P/Citi 500 Value −20.85%	S&P/Citi 500 Value 31.79%	Russell 2000 Growth 14.31%	Russell 2000 4.55%	S&P 500 15.79%	S&P 500 5.49%
Russell 2000 Value 25.75%	Russell 2000 Growth 11.32%	Russell 2000 Growth 12.93%	Russell 2000 Growth 1.23%	S&P/Citi 500 Value 12.73%	MSCI EAFE −14.17%	S&P 500 −11.89%	S&P 500 −22.10%	S&P 500 28.68%	S&P 500 10.88%	Russell 2000 Growth 4.15%	Russell 2000 Growth 13.35%	S&P/Citi 500 Value 1.99%
LB Agg 18.46%	MSCI EAFE 6.05%	LB Agg 9.64%	Russell 2000 −2.55%	LB Agg −0.82%	S&P/Citi 500 Growth −22.08%	S&P/Citi 500 Growth −12.73%	S&P/Citi 500 Growth −23.59%	S&P/Citi 500 Growth 25.66%	S&P/Citi 500 Growth 6.13%	S&P/Citi 500 Growth 4.00%	S&P/Citi 500 Growth 11.01%	Russell 2000 −1.57%
MSCI EAFE 11.21%	LB Agg 3.64%	MSCI EAFE 1.78%	Russell 2000 Value −6.45%	Russell 2000 Value −1.49%	Russell 2000 Value −22.43%	MSCI EAFE −21.44%	Russell 2000 Growth −30.26%	LB Agg 4.10%	LB Agg 4.34%	LB Agg 2.43%	LB Agg 4.33%	Russell 2000 Value −9.78%

FIGURE 9.1 Callan Periodic Table of Investment Returns (1988–2007).
Source: Callan Associates, Inc.

the bottom of the list. For the next seven years, the S&P/Citi 500 Growth class was the second worst performer of all the asset classes.

This rotation of money in and out of asset classes can be seen throughout the 20-year period. From 1989 to 1992, the MSCI EAFE Index, which tracks international stocks, was the worst performer. In 1993 and 1994, the asset class was head and shoulders above its peers, leading the group. The following three years, the MSCI EAFE Index moved back down to the underachievers' territory.

The phenomenon of asset classes not continuing as the leaders for long is an essential part of investing and trading. Even though as swing traders you will not be fixated on the long-term movement of monies, understanding the concept of asset class rotation can improve your success rate. (See Figure 9.2.)

For example, heading into 1993, it was clear nobody was favoring the international stocks, which had been one of the worst performing asset classes. But as soon as the class began to turn around, the charts would

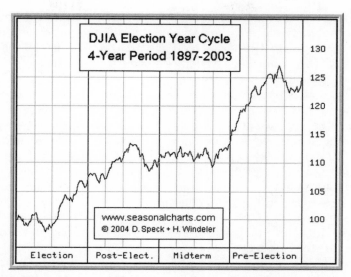

FIGURE 9.2 Dow Jones Four-Year Election Cycle Returns (1897–2003).
Source: www.seasonalcharts.com

have brought to your attention the fact that international stocks were due for a move up the list, and buying opportunities could have arisen.

MARKET CYCLES

The Presidential Election Cycle

One of the most widely followed and well-known stock market cycles involves the four-year term of the U.S. president. The theory behind the four-year cycle is that the market will do well heading into the presidential election, only to falter after the new president takes office or continues his term. In Figure 9.2, the returns for each of the four years within a presidential term (election year, postelection year, midterm year, and preelection year) are charted for the time period of 1897 to 2003.

What is the psychology behind the election cycle returns? In the election year, the president is either new in office or has just begun his second term. Because the candidate has promised a laundry list of changes from the prior president or term, it often results in a number of new bills being passed. To pay for the changes, there is often a change in taxes, and that is never good for Wall Street. There is also the thought process that a new president is unknown, and that could lead to skepticism among investors. When investors are uneasy about a situation or uncertain about the future, they would rather sell first and ask questions later. This is why the election year starts out slow before moving higher as it closes in on the postelection year.

The postelection and midterm election years are not the most exciting times for investors because this is when the government is taking the actions it had promised investors. It is far enough past the most recent election and far enough away from the next election that the president does not have to put the economy on the front burner. The president will probably focus on the agenda for the party and not concentrate as much on how it may look in the eyes of the voters. Therefore, the economy and stock market tend to lag during the middle two years.

The preelection year is when the big gains come for investors. The returns from the low of the midterm election year to the high of the preelection year are the best snapshot of a time frame within the cycle. The buying of stocks during the midterm election year is not a secret on Wall Street, and the media have been making it even more popular the last two elections. With the expansion of the Internet, everyone now has access to the stock cycles that only the pros knew about in the past.

Big gains during the preelection year are driven by the incumbent party trying to keep either the president or their party in the White House. The economy and stock market are always among the leading motives for a voter to choose a candidate. If the party currently in office can show voters a strong economy and a stock market that is performing well, it has a leg up on the competition. The government may offer tax incentives, or the Federal Reserve may preach an attractive monetary policy. Whatever the reason may be, the stock market historically does well the year before an election. The next preelection year will be 2011.

Figures 9.3 through 9.6 show breakdowns of the four years in the presidential election cycle month by month since 1897.

The Best Six Months of the Year

I am sure you have heard "Sell in May and go away." It may bring a smirk to your face, but in reality investors over the years who have done just that have much more than smirks on their faces; they are smiling from ear to ear as they swim in their money.

In the stock market, the best six months of the year for investing begin in November and end in April. The worst six months of the year begin in May and run through October, hence the sell in May adage. Over the years, this has been a very useful tool for investors, but recently it has not been as

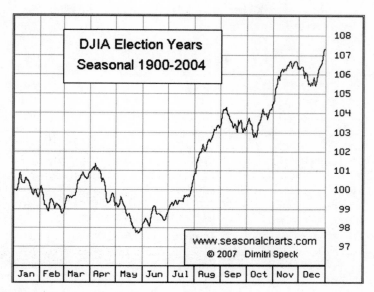

FIGURE 9.3 Dow Jones Election Year (1900–2004).
Source: www.seasonalcharts.com

accurate. Some blame this on the fact that everyone knows about the two six-month time frames, and therefore it will no longer work. However you look at it, there is still some validity to the cycle, and it is tough to argue with the numbers.

According to the *Stock Trader's Almanac*, $10,000 invested in the Dow stocks during the best six months of the year would have grown to $544,323 from 1950 through 2006. During the worst six months of the year, the money was switched to fixed-income investments. If an investor would have taken $10,000 and gone the opposite way and invested in the Dow stocks during the worst six months of the year and fixed income during the best six months of the year, it would have resulted in a loss of $272. This is not just a subtle difference; it is astronomical in magnitude. We are talking hundreds of thousands of dollars and thousands of percentage points of difference.

If you would have followed this best six months cycle during the last four cycles, you would have been disappointed. In 2006 and 2007, the sell in May theory did not work well. The Dow averaged gains of 6.5 percent over the six-month period, which is not great, but certainly not bad. During the best six months, the Dow was flat, gaining 8 percent in 2006–2007 and

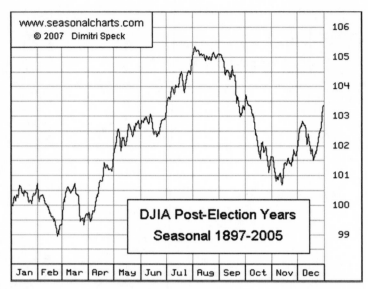

FIGURE 9.4 Dow Jones Postelection Year (1897–2005)
Source: www.seasonalcharts.com

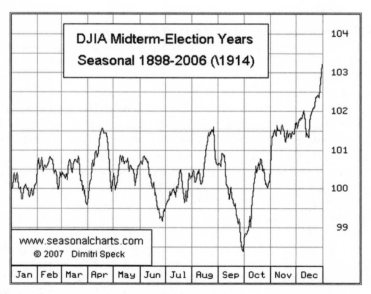

FIGURE 9.5 Dow Jones Midterm Year (1898–2006)
Source: www.seasonalcharts.com

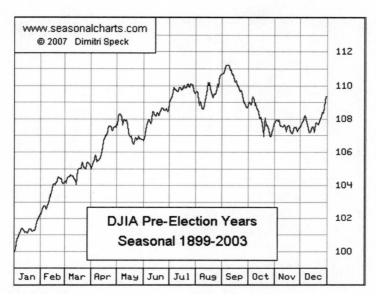

FIGURE 9.6 Dow Jones Preelection Year (1899–2003)
Source: www.seasonalcharts.com

losing 8 percent in 2007–2008. This cycle is more fun than anything else for traders, but again every little piece of information you have about the market and the psychology behind the other traders can make you more successful.

In Figure 9.7, the stock market is shown from 1982 through 2000, which happened to be one of the best periods in the history of the market. During this time, it is evident in the chart that investors made the majority of their money from November through April. From May through October, the index is little changed, and investors would have been better off sitting on the sidelines instead of taking the risk.

SHORT-TERM SECTOR ROTATION

A trade that has been in the market for a few years involves money flowing from one group of sectors to another when the market changes direction. With the commodities being one of the hottest sectors for a few years, when the money begins to flow their way, it does not stop for weeks. However, when the selling begins, it can create a rush for the exits as traders sell and look for a new sector to buy. The beneficiary of any commodity

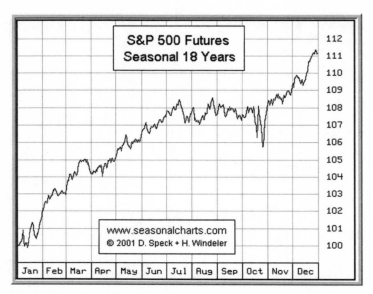

FIGURE 9.7 S&P 500 Monthly Returns
Source: www.seasonalcharts.com

sell-offs in 2007 and 2008 has been the large-cap technology stocks. Traders who crave risk search for the best reward opportunities when they are sitting on cash, and this has led them to rotate money from sector to sector more often in the last few years.

Appetite for quick gains and individual investors' increased access to trading have led to a spike in volatility in the last few years. From day to day, stocks can move several percentage points without raising a red flag for anyone. The volatility has been priced into the market, and therefore traders are now expecting big moves on a daily basis and search for stocks that will give them just that. This is why the money rotates from sector to sector in a short period of time. Traders realize when a sector has made its short-term move and immediately begin looking for the next sector that could be ripe for a move, either to the upside or the downside.

An example of the rotation of money from sector to sector was evident during the fourth quarter of 2007. Big money was flowing into high-volatility areas such as the emerging markets, in particular, China. Figure 9.8 shows the rise of the iShares FTSE/Xinhua China 25 ETF (FXI) from August through October. The appetite for high volatility was prevalent, and what better place to look than Chinese stocks? But when the momentum began to slow, as fast as traders got into the Chinese stocks, they exited even quicker.

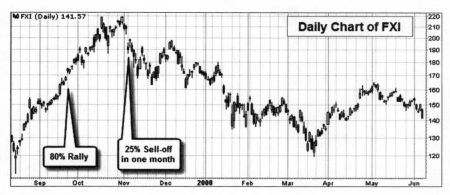

FIGURE 9.8   Sector Rotation in and out of China (FXI)
Source: Chart courtesy of StockCharts.com

Figure 9.9 shows how the SPDRs Select Sector Utilities ETF (XLU) held up much better during the sell-off of China and most sectors in the United States and abroad. As money rotated out of the high-risk sectors such as China, it had to go somewhere, and what better place to go than the utility stocks, which are perceived as a safe haven in times of stock market unrest? Other sectors that typically do well in that type of environment are the drug and health care sectors.

In the last couple of years, a new trading vehicle has been introduced to help investors take advantage of the short-term rotation of money from sector to sector. ETFs that allow investors to profit from drops in certain sectors are referred to as short ETFs. There are even leveraged short ETFs

FIGURE 9.9   Sector Rotation in and out of the Utilities (XLU)
Source: Chart courtesy of StockCharts.com

that offer traders double the inverse of the underlying index. In the time FXI fell 25 percent, the ProShares UltraShort Financials ETF (SKF), which is a leveraged short ETF, gained 40 percent. In Figure 9.10, the charts show how SKF rallied as FXI and the market fell. We discuss the short and ultra-short ETFs in a later chapter.

DOW THEORY

The Dow theory is one of the oldest technical analysis strategies still implemented today and used by the masses. Not only do technical analysts follow the Dow theory, but so do the media and nearly every trader, regardless of strategy. The Dow theory may not be the quintessential sector rotation instrument; however, it did set the stage for several of the popular rotation theories. Therefore, this section highlights how a simple theory is still used today and its importance for swing traders.

Charles Dow is credited with the Dow theory, but he never used that term. After his death, some of his colleagues compiled 255 editorials Dow had written for the *Wall Street Journal* and came up with the basis of the Dow theory. An interesting side note is that Charles Dow was the founder and editor of the *Wall Street Journal,* as well as cofounder of Dow Jones and Company.[1]

There are six basic tenets of the Dow theory.

- The market has three movements (trends).
- Trends have three phases.

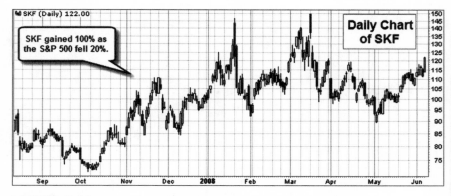

FIGURE 9.10 Outperformance of SKF during Market Sell-Off
Source: Chart courtesy of StockCharts.com

- The stock market discounts all news.
- Stock market averages must confirm each other.
- Trends are confirmed by volume.
- Trends exist until definitive signals prove they have ended.[2]

The three movements are the main movement, medium swing, and short swing. The medium swing is what all swing traders are searching for. According to the Dow theory, the medium swing can last anywhere from 10 days to three months. Never count on a movement lasting more than a month, but then again, if the trend continues and you are making money, let it ride.

The Dow theory believes all trends have three phases: accumulation, public participation, and distribution. Most investment strategies believe in phases of a trend and are typically similar to the three in the Dow theory. For a swing trader, the long side is normally played during the public participation phase because this is when the stock is moving with momentum and probably breaking out to new highs. Ideally, a swing trader prefers to get long during the accumulation phase before the big rally begins in the public participation phase. One of the best indicators to identify accumulation is volume. When big volume is coming into a stock on up days, it could be a signal that smart money is accumulating shares of the stock before a breakout.

The stock market discounts all news. This may or may not be true, depending on whom you ask. I personally feel the majority of the time the news is discounted in a stock, and the market is efficient. However, there are instances when smart money (or illegal money) knows things they should not, and the stock is not acting efficiently. Again, this is where volume can play a key role.

Stock market averages must confirm each other. This is the part of the Dow theory that gets the most media time. The theory holds that there cannot be a bull market with both the Dow Jones Industrial Average and the Dow Jones Transportation Average in uptrends. The concept goes back to the day when Charles Dow believed the transportation stocks (railroads at the time) could not trade independently of the industrials in a bull market. How could the rails not do well when trains were needed to ship the increased demand for industrials? One sector could not do well without the help of the other. When the two were diverging, it was a troublesome sign, and when they came back together in conjoining uptrends, it was bullish for the market.

Trends are confirmed by volume. This is one of the cornerstones of my investing strategy. There is no chance of a rally turning into a sustainable long-term uptrend without big volume behind it. The lack of volume suggests the market is being moved by a small portion of traders/investors and that the buying will fade out quickly after it begins. This concept is also used during a sell-off; if the selling is on light volume, it is actually bullish for the market.

Trends exist until definitive signals prove they have ended. When I refer to this concept, my wording is a bit different: The trend is your friend, until it ends. As swing traders, we like to stay with the main trend and trade in that direction if at all possible. That being said, there are times when swing traders can take advantage of countertrend moves with tight stop losses. At the end of the day, the majority of your trades should be in the direction of the trend until it ends. Trying to prematurely pick the top of an uptrend or the bottom of a downtrend can be disastrous to your bottom line and is not suggested. Simply remember the rhyme, and you'll be on the right track.

CHAPTER 10

Strategy 6: The Macro-to-Micro Play

How the Broad Indices Can Help You Beat the Market

There are two general strategies for breaking down the thousands of stocks in the market. The more popular of the two is a bottom-up approach that begins by analyzing the individual stock, regardless of what is going on around it. The alternative is a top-down approach that begins by analyzing the overall market before moving on to sectors and finally individual stocks. I can make a case for both strategies in certain situations. However, if a trader is willing to put in the time to find the best trading setups, the top-down strategy is the best option.

The top-down approach, as it is called on the street, will be referred to as our macro-to-micro (M-to-M) strategy for the remainder of the book. The argument most often heard against the M-to-M is that it is better suited for investors versus traders. While this may be true, the strategy can also help traders build a watchlist of stocks that can take advantage of the current overall market and direct them to the best reward-to-risk sectors.

To prove the M-to-M strategy can be helpful for traders, we can analyze the performance of the S&P 500 and its components during the first quarter of 2008. The S&P 500 fell 10 percent during the first three months of 2008, making it the worst quarter in four years. As you can imagine, it was difficult for traders to make money going long, and there were many more opportunities for short selling. At the end of the quarter, only 117 of the 500 stocks in the S&P 500 closed higher; making the probability of picking a winner for the entire sector a mere 23 percent.

Granted, there are many tradable swings throughout the quarter on both the long and short sides, but it is clear that the path of least resistance was lower and the big money was made by shorting the weak stocks. When using the M-to-M approach, we are able to identify the trend of the overall market (in this case, the S&P 500) and use it to plan the direction of the majority of trades. The key is determining the overall trend and then trading in the direction of the trend to increase the probability of winning trades.

To give you an insight into how the M-to-M approach can be used for investors, the following is from an article I wrote for investopedia.com in 2007.

> *Because the top-down approach begins at the top, the first step is to determine the health of the world economy. This is done by analyzing not only the developed countries of North America and Western Europe, but also emerging countries in Latin America and Asia. A quick way to determine the health of an economy is by looking at the GDP growth of the past few years and the estimates going forward. Often times the emerging market countries will have the best growth numbers when compared with its mature counterparts. Unfortunately we live at a time where war and geopolitical tensions are heightened; therefore we must also not forget to be mindful of what is currently affecting each region of the world.*
>
> *There will naturally be a few regions and countries throughout the world that will immediately fall off the radar and will no longer be included in the remainder of the analysis. After determining which regions present a high reward-to-risk ratio, the next step is to use the charts and technical analysis. By looking at a long-term chart of the specific countries stock index we can determine if the corresponding stock market is in an uptrend and worth further time or a downtrend and not an appropriate place to put our money at this time.*
>
> *The next step is to analyze more in-depth the economy of the United States along with the health of the stock market in particular. By examining the economic numbers such as interest rates, inflation, and employment number we are able to determine the current strength of the market and have a better idea of what the future holds. There is often a divergence between the story the economic numbers tell and the trend of the stock market indices.*

This makes the logical next step the analysis of the major U.S. stock indices such as the S&P 500 and NASDAQ Composite. Both fundamental and technical analysis are used as barometers to determine the health of the indices. The fundamentals of the market can be determined by such ratios as price to earnings, price to sales, and dividend yields. Comparing the numbers to past readings can help to determine if the market is at a level that is historically overbought or oversold. Technical analysis can help to ascertain where the market is in relation to the long-term cycle. Charts that show the past several decades are used, and eventually the time horizon is zoned down to a daily view. Indicators such as the 50-day and 200-day moving averages help us find the current trend of the market and decide if it is appropriate for investors to be heavily invested in equities.

STEP-BY-STEP MACRO-TO-MICRO APPROACH FOR SWING TRADERS

1. Analyze the current global trend.
   a. Determine the trend of the major U.S. indices.
   b. Determine the trend of the MSCI EAFE Index.
   c. Determine the trend of the MSCI Emerging Markets Index.
   d. If two of the three indices are trending higher, the global trend will be considered bullish.
2. Analyze the U.S. asset classes individually.
   a. Determine the trend of the Russell 1000 Value Index.
   b. Determine the trend of the Russell 1000 Growth Index.
   c. Determine the trend of the S&P 600 Small-Cap Index.
   d. Determine the trend of the S&P 400 Mid-Cap Index.
   e. If the global trend in number 1 has been determined to be bullish, the strongest of these four indices will be the first index analyzed for potential buying opportunities.
   f. If the global trend in number 1 has been determined to be bearish, the weakest of these four indices will be the first index analyzed for potential short opportunities.
3. Analyze the sectors by using technical analysis.
   a. Identify the strongest sectors in the marketplace by analyzing the trend of the charts.
4. Analyze the individual stocks within the sectors that were chosen in number 3 and begin to build a watchlist of tradable candidates.
5. Determine the entry and exit parameters for the watchlist of stocks, and when the entry prices are hit, initiate the trades.

THE DAILY MACRO-TO-MICRO TRADE STRATEGY

Every trader's dream is to know the news before everyone else. Unfortunately, the only way to accomplish this is to get tomorrow's newspaper today, which unless you have the flux capacitor from *Back to the Future*, is not going to happen. Another way involves having inside information and trading on it—something I will assume your ethical boundaries will keep you from participating in.

The closest thing to tomorrow's newspaper I have found has been the daily macro-to-micro trade. This strategy uses the news that you know and takes into consideration its full effect on the market and individual stocks.

For example, assume company ABC comes out with earnings before the bell and blows the estimates out of the water. The stock rises 10 percent in premarket trading as investors cheer the numbers and rush to buy the stock. The majority of the time it is too late to buy ABC stock because the move has already been made. However, what about other stocks in the same business as ABC? Assume ABC is a construction machinery producer, and they attributed their better-than-expected earnings to the strong demand globally for construction machinery. If ABC is seeing strong demand around the globe for their products, other companies selling construction machinery are also apt to see increased demand, thus resulting in higher sales and eventually better-than-expected earnings. Because all the attention has been placed on ABC stock, its competitors have been put on the back burner, and most traders are ignoring them in the early hours of trading.

However, if you are able to find other companies that have businesses similar to ABC, you will be ahead of the curve and can begin buying before the other traders. Eventually, other traders and investors will catch on to the idea and see ABC's competitors begin to move higher, thus creating a mad buying frenzy for the other stocks in the sector. The key is getting there early and being at the leading edge of the news.

A trader need a real-time news service that provides earnings reports as soon as they are released. A web site service that I use and believe is one of the better around is www.briefing.com. The real-time streaming news does cost money, but as you already know, it takes money to make money.

There are two approaches a trader can take to this strategy. The first involves simply watching the news wire and when you see a stock-moving headline cross, begin the process of seeing if the stock is moving on the news. If the stock is a viable candidate, the next step is to find competitors in the same sector that will be affected by the news.

The second approach is usually the more reliable and definitely less hectic way of playing the daily news. A trader can do research ahead of time by getting a list of stocks that are reporting earnings the following day or are speaking at an investment conference. Narrowing the list to a few stocks you think will release market-moving news and gathering the competitors that could move as well form the basis of the research. The trader must then look for the news to hit the wires and make the appropriate trades based on the movement of the stock releasing the news. This approach results in a more systematic approach to the daily M-to-M play and helps to eliminate making emotional decisions because of a lack of time spent on research.

Daily Macro-to-Micro Example

On April 2, 20008, the well-known electronics retailer Best Buy (BBY) reported quarterly earnings that were better than the street's estimate, and the stock immediately began to rise. The report hit the wires before the bell, and the premarket price of BBY stock reflected the news within seconds of the press release. Figure 10.1 displays the move in the price of Best Buy. An astute swing trader would have checked the earnings reports scheduled for the premarket, and with only a few slated to report that day, I am sure Best Buy would have made the list. The trader would have then looked for direct competitors that could be affected by either good news or bad news regarding sales and future guidance. Because Best Buy is in a niche marketplace, its direct competitor is Circuit City (CC). But there is also another company that began trading on the NYSE in 2007, hhgregg, Inc. (HGG). The majority of its electronics stores, which resemble Best Buy stores, are located east of the Mississippi River. What makes the find of HGG so great is that not many people have ever heard of the company, and therefore it should go unnoticed for a long enough time to make a trade before it begins to rally on the Best Buy news.

The HGG stock opened the trading day at $11.80, 12 cents higher than the $11.68 close from the previous session (Figure 10.2). The first hour saw the stock move sideways with an intraday low of $11.70. Then the move

FIGURE 10.1 Chart of Best Buy
Source: Chart courtesy of StockCharts.com

FIGURE 10.2   Chart of hhgregg
Source: Chart courtesy of StockCharts.com

began, just at 11:00 A.M. ET, and shot up to $12.25. The 45 cent move from
the open of $11.80 is a quick 3.8 percent profit for the traders who were
willing to do a little extra work and find HGG in the research. When traders
can spot stocks that are not mainstream, they have time to get into a trade
at a reasonable price without chasing a stock that gaps higher. HGG gave
traders plenty of time to enter the trade in the first two hours of trading
and, a couple of hours later, exit with a nice one-day profit.

CHAPTER 11

Strategy 7: Profit from Exuberance Premium

There's an old adage in the market that says, "People don't have to buy—ever. But they do have to sell sometime." This is why stocks usually climb slowly, over time—and then when bad news surfaces, they scream downward at a breakneck speed, especially after a big upside run. It's pretty simple, actually. After a stock has moved up substantially, when the tide turns, many investors quickly rush to sell shares to ensure they don't lose profit, or principal.

What's more, there's another old piece of market knowledge that explains why stocks tear downward, the greater fool theory. What this means is that when you buy a stock, there has to be a greater fool out there to buy the stock higher. The theory explains two things.

- When stocks move up, investors do often act foolishly, buying at extremely high levels, even though the stock is overvalued. This is what we call *exuberance*.
- Why do stocks turn down quickly after a large run? The simple fact of the matter is that the market has finally run out of fools. And when the last fool is finally in, look out below!

This chapter covers how to spot overbought stocks. Many swing traders know that finding—and shorting—heavily overbought stocks can be one of the most profitable activities within the market. What's more, because overbought stocks sell off so quickly, often the hold times can be minimal, especially when average investor selling is further fueled by institutions or funds forced to completely bail. It's important to take extra care to note that there is danger in attempting to trade overbought stocks, as we are truly "trading against the trend." Doing so involves more risk than usual, as we are not only attempting to bet against momentum, but exuberance as well. As John Maynard Keynes said, "The market can stay exuberant longer than you can stay solvent." What's more, Alan Greenspan coined the term "irrational exuberance" in the dot.bomb era. With these two insights in mind, we want to be cognizant of the possibility of extended exuberance, so as to not to step in front of a moving bus on the highway. However, with a little caution and care, we can jump on the torrid bulls, just as their "irrational exuberance" is running out of steam, while keeping our stops tight enough to ensure our solvency over the long haul.

These special situations yield mega profits very quickly.

TECHNICALS TELL A TON

We're using technicals as our first filter to find overbought stocks. Then we use technicals as confirmation of trade entry, after we've verified that the stock is fundamentally overbought. Really, we're using commonsense fundamentals to confirm these trades, though technicals play a large part in finding and entering them as well. Thus, we will start with technicals to locate potentially overbought scenarios.

As we begin to look through various sectors for overbought situations, we're going to use a few simple technical tools to help us locate stocks that could be overbought, meaning exuberance has driven them to unsustainable levels, at least in the short-term anyway.: the 200-SMA, stochastics, and on balance volume (OBV).

The 200-SMA

Why moving averages? The simple answer is that moving averages—especially the 200-SMA—are a great way to determine if a stock is trading substantially off its mean. And as descriptive statistics prove again and again, everything always returns to the mean; it's only a matter of how long it will take. As a general rule of thumb, when a stock, or index, begins to trade around 20 percent, or more above the 200-SMA, put it on your radar for a reversal.

Stochastics

As a general definition, stochastics indicate overbought (and oversold) stocks by measuring the close prices in relation to the highs of the day.

When prices continually close at highs, intuitively we know the stock is moving higher. Thus, as stochastics near the top of the range, we can assume that buying momentum has been stronger than normal and that the stock may be entering overbought territory. It's important to note that we are not using stochastics as an "indicator" of trade entry, rather, we are using stochastics as a guidance tool to attempt to find some indication that the stock, ETF, or index is nearing the top of the range.

On Balance Volume (OBV)

OBV is a great indicator of overbought stocks, as it measures the amount of buying volume versus selling volume. The concept is painfully simple: When there is substantially more buying in a stock than selling, OBV rises (and in theory, so should the stock.) Conversely, when selling volume begins to taper, OBV falls within its oscillator range. Although OBV may seem all too simple, the indicator is actually a great tool, especially for longer-term trends. OBV is an oscillator fluctuating between 0 and 100. When OBV begins to retrace itself from overbought (top) and oversold (bottom) levels of the indicator window, it can sometimes foreshadow the actual movement of the stock. For OBV to drop dramatically, the stock needs to drop as well; however, during times of lateral movement, or indicator window retracement, the scenarios can give us hints that the momentum within our trade just isn't for real. In other words, in a lateral range where the stock is slowly edging higher, while OBV is waning south, the buying momentum within the stock is likely a glass house about to crumble.

Figure 11.1 shows First Solar, a great company but one that was definitely entering overbought territory in late 2007. As the chart shows, the stock was trading about 130 percent above the 200-SMA, while also witnessing overbought OBV and stochastics. The technical events at hand would have been a strong signal to look into the company's fundamentals—and current events—to attempt to unearth why the stock had been rallying so, and whether the upward move was entering exuberance territory. The point of the previous chart is simply to show how we identify when exuberance has set in and how we spot the irrationality at hand. Of course, actually trading the exuberance premium is whole other story, which we will cover in just a moment.

IDENTIFYING EXUBERANCE PREMIUM

The primary driver behind why stocks move is often their story, something there was no lack of for First Solar throughout 2007. As global warming

FIGURE 11.1   First Solar (Nasdaq: FSLR) with OBV and Slow Stochastics
Source: Chart courtesy of StockCharts.com

kicked into high gear, many green-related industries like solar energy shot through the roof. First Solar certainly was exactly in one of those sectors that found no lack of buying.

Phoenix-based First Solar was certainly a story stock as well, as investors began to see that the company had positioned itself well within solar markets both in America and internationally, with factories in Malaysia and blistering sales for industrial use in Europe.

What's more, the company began seeing double-digit earnings growth, as sales continued to roll through the door. Moreover, throughout 2007 and 2008, fears began to surface within the solar market that many solar companies would begin to see earnings decline because of rising prices for polysilicon, one of the major building blocks of solar wafers.

What's more, CNBC's Jim Cramer was a huge fan of the company and constantly pumped shares on the tube as a screaming buy. In essence, on the news front, First Solar was in the right place, at the right time, with the right product, with the right media support. It's no wonder shares were boiling upward.

Was First Solar's run into late 2007 a moment of exuberance?

Let's take a look at the fundamentals. In late 2007, full-year EPS estimates for 2008 were around $1.40 a share, while the stock traded around $260 a share mid-December. At that time, the forward PE for 2008 was about 185.

What's more, the company was trading with double-digit price to sales and price to book numbers.

Looking two years out to 2009, full-year EPS was expected at $2.85 a share, more than double 2008 estimates. What this means is that looking out two years, the stock was trading with a forward PE of 91. Let's phrase that a different way: The stock was trading at 91 times expected earnings two years from the actual value in December 2007.

What does common sense tell you?

If you're **not** thinking *exuberance*, fueled by media frenzy and the greater fool theory, we've done a poor job of relaying the concepts in this chapter.

See, those who believe in the stock—and don't get us wrong, First Solar is an incredible company—will tell you that the outlook is so bright, the company could see increased sales and completely blow the doors off future expectations. Those who are emotionally attached to the story believe nothing will go wrong in the future. But here's the problem: So much premium was priced into the stock that it didn't leave *any* room for error at the company, or in the broader market. What's more, if any hiccup in the supply chain, unforeseen natural events, or even political turmoil just whispered danger in the company's direction, so much exuberance premium had been priced into the stock that it was a glass house just waiting for a stone. Keep in mind that by *glass house* we are referring to the stock price, not First Solar as a company. Sadly, while First Solar is a great company, the way Wall Street had run it though the roof was setting the stock up for failure when the last fool had bought in.

Case in point, just at the beginning of 2008, First Solar began to tumble, with the stock falling almost 42 percent from highs in the $280 area (Figure 11.2). Those who know how to find overbought stocks probably profited handsomely from the event; those who bought the highs are probably still griping about the massive chunk of cash they lost in the trade.

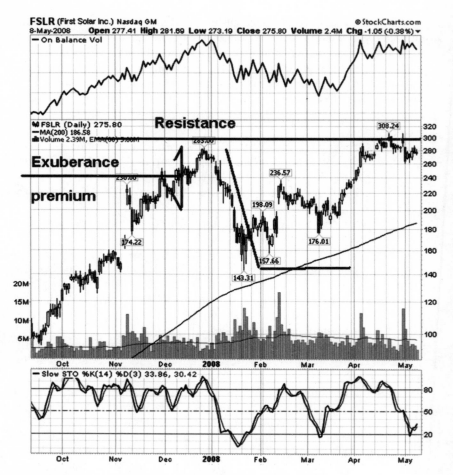

FIGURE 11.2   First Solar Showing Resistance and Exuberance
Source: Chart courtesy of StockCharts.com

It should be clear that we're not doing a ton of complicated fundamental analysis here. We're simply using commonsense fundamental ratios to identify an exuberance premium. **In fact, as a general rule of thumb, if you see a PE over 80, you should immediately consider the possibility of whether the exuberance paradigm is setting in.** A PE of 50 is still very high, though many analysts who never have to put their money where their own mouths are will tell you that high PEs signify growth and/or are consummate with a blossoming industry, often technology related. There's a difference between growth and exuberance, which is why time and time again investors get hurt buying story stocks with unrealistic ratios.

TECHNICAL ENTRY AND RISK MANAGEMENT

Within this chapter, we've clearly outlined why and how identifying over-bought stocks can help you avoid making the huge mistake of buying something that's about to fall through the floor. We have also identified the other side of the coin: the fact that massively overbought stocks could be huge short winners for savvy swing traders. The question, though, when trading exuberance short, is how and where the last fool will be in?

To answer the question, we must almost throw fundamentals out the door, as the market pretty much already has too. Thus, once we've identified that a stock has become fundamentally exuberant; timing an entry short can often be found via technical analysis. In the case of First Solar, investors who were looking at the stock in November 2007 probably would have been tempted to go short. However, if they had, in the $200 to $220 area, they would have probably been killed. But here's the thing: Even though the stock was up over 100 percent since October, both stochastics and OBV weren't showing capitulation just yet. The simple fact of the matter is that when trading exuberance, we want stochastics and OBV virtually pegged out at 100. Make no exceptions, because we're trading one of the riskiest situations in the market: We're shorting the scenario where investors have completely lost their minds.

Notice, though, that in December, First Solar attempted one last break-out, rallying up to $283. There was one very critical piece of information that could have alerted short traders that it was time to get in. What savvy bears knew was that the stock was trading just shy of a huge whole number.

In late December, when the stock was trading at $280 a share, the difference between the stock price and $300 a share was 7 percent. However, the stock was trading almost 60 percent above the 200-SMA.

Hopefully, you're seeing the picture come together.

- The stock was fundamentally overbought.
- Investor exuberance was at highs, as fools were pricing in never-ending earnings growth.
- The media was making the situation worse.
- Stochastics and OBV were painfully overbought.
- The stock was trading 130 percent above the 200-SMA, which translates to a 60 percent bomb from $280 a share.
- The stock was sitting just below a huge whole number that was likely to serve as resistance.
- Using the whole number as a stop, short investors would risk 6 percent, while potentially earning 60 percent.

I don't think there's much left to question. Clearly, the stock tanked, because those who are savvy on Wall Street knew: What goes up must always come down eventually.

Sadly, at the time we were writing this book, First Solar had once again fired up to sky-high levels. Future estimates were showing that the stock could run even higher as the exuberance premium once again builds. We're guessing First Solar could run as high as $360 to $390 a share before investors figure out they are in the middle of an exuberance minefield created by Wall Street.

Because First Solar is truly a great company, too, it is truly sad to see that bulls could care less. At the end of the day, while incredible companies often see Wall Street ramp up exuberance within the underlying stock, pullbacks come fast and hard for those who buy recklessly.

Next, we'll cover technical trading with Japanese candlestick charting, which, when used properly, can be a very powerful tool that helps you identify bold trading opportunities. What's more, as you're about to see, understanding candlestick charting can help with both our technical entries and the overall risk management within our trades.

CHAPTER 12

Strategy 8: Japanese Candlestick Charts

T o the uneducated eye a Japanese candlestick chart can look foreign and overwhelming. There are shadows and bodies and dojis and even haramis to deal with. Why would anyone want to use the candlestick chart versus a normal bar chart? For starters, the Japanese candlesticks are built by using the same information that constructs a bar chart: the open, close, high, and low of the day. Second, many active traders consider themselves visual people, and the candlestick charts are great for traders who can visualize patterns. Finally, the Japanese have been using the candlestick charting system for centuries.

The candlestick is made up of the open, close, high, and low of any given period. The candlestick charts can be used on a daily, weekly, or even 1-minute chart, similar to bar charts. Figure 12.1 shows how the four prices are incorporated in the construction of the candlestick. The open and close are represented by the body of the candlestick. On a day when the open is higher than the close, the open is the top of the body. When the close is higher than the open, the close is the upper end of the body. The top of the upper shadow always represents the high of the day, and the lowest point of the lower shadow is the low of the day.

To differentiate an up day from a down day, the body can be either white or black. When the body is white, as it is in Figure 12.1, the close is higher than the open, suggesting the stock closed higher than its opening price. When the body is black, it represents a down day, and the upper end of the body is the open and the lower end is the close. There are also some trading systems and web sites that replace white with green and black with red. I tend to go with the old-school black and white, but many traders appreciate the color scheme.

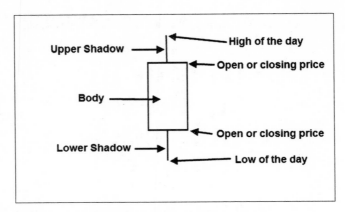

FIGURE 12.1 Anatomy of a Japanese Candlestick

The shadows, also referred to as *wicks* or *tails*, can vary greatly in length and may not even appear in certain situations. If the stock opens on the low of the day and closes on the high of the day, there is only a body, with no shadows. This is rare, but it does occur, and you should be aware that it is possible when you are looking at the charts.

When it comes to using the candlesticks for swing trading, traders must realize that there are two ways to approach the charts. The first involves looking solely at the individual candle, and the action on that one day tells you about the stock. The second approach requires the trader to look at a series of candlesticks to determine if a tradable pattern has formed, possibly signaling a buy or sell. Throughout this chapter, we highlight a number of individual candlesticks that are important for swing traders to comprehend, as well as multicandlestick patterns that generate buy and sell signals.

SINGLE CANDLESTICK PATTERNS

Doji

The doji is one of the most popular and useful candlesticks for two reasons: It is easily identifiable, and it often signals trend reversals. The doji is a candle that has little or no body (Figure 12.2). It occurs when the open and close are at or near the same price. Think about what it means to have the open and close at the same price after the stock trades lower and higher throughout the session. The significance behind the doji is that it represents a struggle between the buyers and sellers during the trading

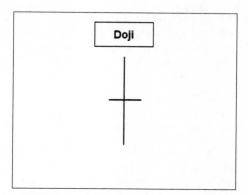

FIGURE 12.2 Doji Pattern

day, and at the end the result is a draw; the stock ended at the same price as it began.

The reason the doji often signals the end of the current short-term trend is that instead of the buyers being in control during an uptrend or the sellers dominating a downtrend, the doji indicates no clear leader in the market. When a doji appears during an uptrend, it signals that the bulls may be losing their handle on the market and the bears are gaining control. During a downtrend, a doji signals that the bears are weakening and the bulls are beginning to come back into the market. Granted, the doji represents only one day's worth of action, but the candlestick is one of the most powerful one-day patterns. Sometimes though, it's always important to use "confirmation" with dojis (or any other candlestick pattern for that matter), meaning the candle following the "indicator candle" should confirm the previous signal. Imaging that at the top of a range a doji appears, whereby tons of traders step in with short positions. Then, the following morning the stock gaps up based on a takeover rumor. The problem is that because the following day presents higher trading action, the short sell doji signal was actually a head fake. However, if traders had waited for a lower low the day following the doji, the indecision (and potential top presented by the doji) would have been confirmed. Remember: confirmation is key.

Other things to consider when looking at a doji are the size of the shadows. A long shadow on the downside indicates that the price of the stock was much lower at one point in the day and that the stock rallied to close off the lows; this is a bullish pattern. When the shadow on the upside is long, it indicates that the stock closed well off the intraday highs and that the bears might be gaining control. When both shadows are long, the candle is referred to as a long-legged doji, and it tells the trader that the bulls and bears are very uncertain. If the open and close happen on the high of the day and there is only a shadow on the downside, the candle is referred to as a dragonfly doji. The opposite of the dragonfly doji is the gravestone doji; there is a shadow on only the upside of the open/close line. Throughout the chapter, you will encounter multicandle patterns that include the doji.

Hammer, Hanging Man, and Shooting Star

If the body of the candlestick is bigger than the line on the doji, yet small relative to a normal body size, it represents a number of possible candlesticks. When a candlestick has a small body, it is referred to as a spinning top. The spinning top can have the small body anywhere on the candle, and there are no further restrictions. The theory behind a spinning top is similar to a doji in that it is a possible reversal signal.

When the small body appears at the top or bottom of the candlestick, it tells more of a story, and there are names for the different placements. A candlestick with a small body at the top and a shadow on the downside is referred to as a hammer when it appears during a downtrend and called a hanging man at the top of an uptrend. A candlestick with the small body at the bottom of the candle and a shadow on the upside is referred to as a shooting star. If you take a look at the illustrations of the three candlestick patterns (Figures 12.3 to 12.5), you can see how the names match the formations.

Similar to the doji, the three candlesticks illustrated (hammer, hanging man, and shooting star) are used extensively in the multicandle patterns in this chapter.

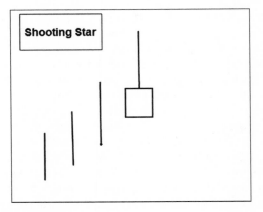

FIGURE 12.3 Shooting Star

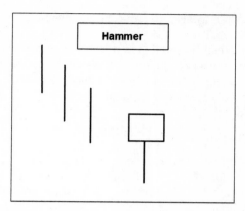

FIGURE 12.4   Hammer

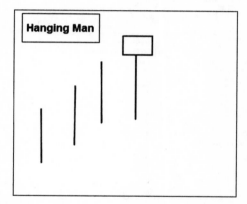

FIGURE 12.5   Hanging Man

Belt Holds

So far, we have been discussing candlesticks with small or no bodies. They typically are considered trend-reversal candles because they signal indecision in the stock. The belt hold candle is the exact opposite because it has a large body. The bullish belt hold candle opens at or near the low of the day and closes at or near the high of the day. The end result is a large white candle that has little or no shadow. The bearish belt hold candle opens at or near the high of the day and closes at or near the low of the day. The candle resembles the bullish belt hold except it is black because it was a down day. Both candles are strong indicators about where the next short-term trend may be going. When they occur during trends that are opposite the candlestick, they often signal a reversal.

For example, when the bullish belt hold appears during a downtrend, it signifies that the bulls have taken complete control of the stock for the day and that the tides may be changing. Figures 12.6 and 12.7 give you an idea of how the belt holds should appear.

Harami Patterns

The harami patterns are two-candle reversal patterns that help to determine the end of a short-term trend. The requirements of a harami pattern are a large black or white, big-bodied candlestick, followed by a candlestick with a very small body that must trade within the range of the first candlestick's body. The significance of the harami pattern can be separated into two parts: The first candlestick has the stock hitting a new high

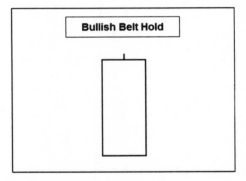

FIGURE 12.6 Bullish Belt Hold

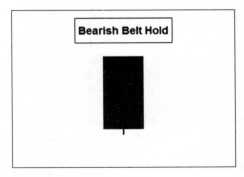

FIGURE 12.7 Bearish Belt Hold

during an uptrend and a new low in a downtrend. The second candlestick in the bullish harami pattern fails to get above the prior day's high, suggesting weakness. The second candlestick in the bearish harami pattern fails to break below the low of the prior day, indicating the bears are losing control. Figures 12.8 and 12.9 show the harami patterns.

If the second candlestick is a doji, the pattern is referred to as a harami cross, either bull or bear.

Morning Star and Evening Star

Two of my favorite three-day patterns and in my mind one of the more reliable candlestick patterns for both swing traders and investors are the morning and evening stars. The morning and evening star patterns begin

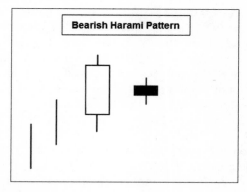

FIGURE 12.8 Bearish Harami

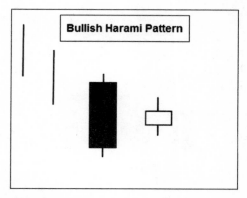

FIGURE 12.9 Bullish Harami

with the trend continuing, followed by indecision in the trend, and ends with a countertrend move.

The morning star pattern occurs when the stock is in the middle of a downtrend, and the first candlestick is a long black candlestick. After day one, the bears believe they are still in control, because they are, and traders do not have the stock on their radar for a potential buy candidate. The second candlestick confirms the bearish tone at the open by gapping down to a new low. Throughout the day, the stock trades, but when it closes, a spinning top is formed, and a candlestick with a small body now sits next to the big black candlestick. The second candle, referred to as the star, is the first inclination the stock is losing its bearish momentum. After gapping down to a new low, the bears were unable to continue pushing the stock lower throughout the day, resulting in a win for the bulls at the closing bell. But before traders can put hard-earned money into buying the stock, confirmation is needed. The third candlestick has a large white body that displays the stock closed well off the lows of the day. The candlestick closes at least halfway into the body of the first candlestick. The confirmation is now in; the bulls are in control, and the short-term downtrend is over.

An evening star is the exact opposite of a morning star. The first candlestick has a large white body that hits a new high. The second candlestick gaps to a new high on the open before closing close to the opening price. The final candlestick has a large black body that closes at least halfway down the body of the first candlestick. Figures 12.10 and 12.11 show examples.

If the second candlestick, also known as the star, is a doji, the pattern will be known as a morning doji star or an evening doji star. I believe the doji in the second day is even more confirmation of a trend reversal, and I put more faith into trading the doji star patterns.

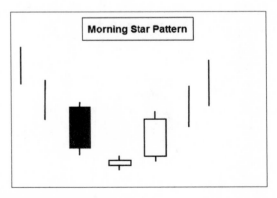

FIGURE 12.10   Morning Star Pattern

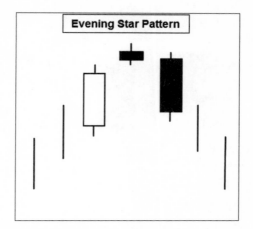

FIGURE 12.11 Evening Star Pattern

Engulfing Patterns

The bullish and bearish engulfing patterns show a two-day pattern. The bullish engulfing pattern occurs when a small candlestick with short shadows is followed by a large white candlestick in which the body encompasses the entire first candlestick. The high and low of the first candlestick fall within the range of the body of the second candlestick. As you can imagine, the second candlestick is extremely bullish because it closes well off the lows of the day. It does this after gapping down to a new low, and by the end of the day, it closes above the intraday high from a day earlier.

The bearish engulfing pattern begins with a small candlestick, typically in an uptrend. The second day, the candlestick opens higher than the previous high and closes below the previous low, creating a large black body that engulfs the entire first candlestick. The two engulfing patterns are typically reliable reversal patterns but can also be used as confirmation that the trend will continue. For example, if a small candlestick (also known as a spinning top) forms during an uptrend, it could be the first signal of the trend changing. However, when the large bullish engulfing candlestick follows the spinning top, it confirms that the first candlestick was merely a one-day event and that the uptrend remains intact.

Two examples of the engulfing patterns are shown in Figures 12.12 and 12.13.

Rising and Falling Three Methods

Nearly every aspect of candlestick charting has revolved around reversal patterns and how to spot the end of a trend. As you know by now, we

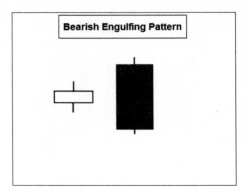

FIGURE 12.12 Bearish Engulfing Pattern

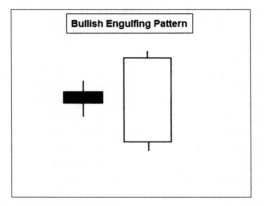

FIGURE 12.13 Bullish Engulfing Pattern

believe following the trend of a stock is one of the basics of a swing trader who relies on momentum trading. The two patterns about to be discussed take five days to be completed and are considered continuation patterns. They confirm the current trend of the stock and give investors reason to hold onto their swing trade or to enter a trade in the direction of the trend. And there is also the possibility that the pattern can keep a trader from going against the trend with an ill-advised trade.

The rising three methods pattern begins with a stock that is in the midst of an uptrend. The first candlestick includes a large white body as the stock hits a new high. The next three candlesticks trend downward, with at least two of the candlesticks having black bodies. The key to the three candlesticks is that they must stay within the range of the white body of the first candlestick. Therefore, the three candlesticks have small bodies and trading ranges. The fifth and final candlestick is another large white body that closes at a new high, above the first candlestick.

The theory behind the rising three methods is that the stock is in the middle of a strong uptrend, as evidenced by the first candlestick's hitting a new high. However, the bulls take a breather, and the stock pulls back for a few days. By holding above the lower end of the body of the first candlestick, the stock shows that the pullback was merely the bulls taking a breather and not the bears taking control. If the three-day pullback is accompanied by light volume, the pattern becomes even more bullish.

The falling three methods pattern is the exact opposite of the rising three methods. The first day is a candlestick with a large black body that is in the midst of a downtrend. The next three days are small-bodied candlesticks that stay within the range of the first candlestick. The rally attempt is thwarted on the fifth day; another candlestick with a large black body closes at a new low.

Figures 12.14 and 12.15 illustrate the two patterns.

WRAPPING UP CANDLESTICKS

This chapter covered the basic one-day candlestick formations and some of the relevant patterns that swing traders can utilize on a daily basis. Even though I believe the Japanese candlestick charts are far superior to bar charts, you do not need to make the change immediately. However, to become a complete swing trader, doing so is a necessity at some point in the future. Just knowing the basics of candlestick charting can help you

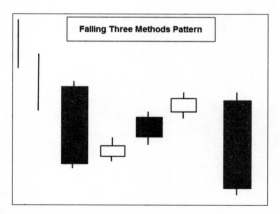

FIGURE 12.14 Falling Three Methods

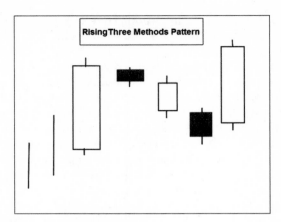

FIGURE 12.15   Rising Three Methods

identify patterns that may be of use in finding trades or keeping you from
entering a poor trade. Simple candlesticks such as the doji, which is very
easy to spot (it was the first candlestick term I learned), can lead to a new
world of trading opportunities. I will bet that after you give the candlesticks
a try, you will never turn back.

Another benefit to the candlestick charting is the synergies that
Western-style technical analysis has with the Eastern style (candlesticks).
When a falling three methods pattern coincides with support on a stock
and bullish volume, the probability of success is about as high as you can
imagine. Once you are able to get a good understanding of both candlestick
charting and Western style, you will become a better trader overnight. Your
brain is a large and powerful tool that has plenty of room for both styles of
technical analysis.

Strategy 9: Option Primer and LEAP Options

Throughout Chapter 13, we're going to cover what options are, what they're used for, and how you can use them to swing trade. Moreover, we also cover LEAP options—which are basically long-term options—discussing why LEAPs can help option investors profit over the long haul. We want you to begin thinking about options now and keep them in the back of your mind while you read Chapters 14 through 17. Then, in Chapters 18, 19, and 20, we specifically discuss options strategies that can return big profits for savvy swing traders.

BRIEF EXPLANATION OF OPTIONS

Options are risky—there's no doubt about it. Most people who trade options lose money, plain and simple. In short, options are the *right*, but not the *obligation*, to buy or sell a stock at a certain price, up to a certain date in time. Imagine it like this: You own an ice cream stand on the corner, and I want to buy it. However, I'm also a little unsure about the present state of affairs in the neighborhood, as lately it seems trouble's been brewing with a gang of kids on the next block over. I think to myself, "I sure would like to own that ice cream stand, but only if the neighborhood stays safe and people feel comfortable walking the streets. Those youngsters on the next block over could wreck the whole thing, especially if the people of the neighborhood start to feel that danger looms." Clearly, buying the ice cream stand is a risk and would require considerable capital outlay.

Then one day, the ice cream guy puts a "For Sale" sign on his stand. You think to yourself, "Wow, I want to buy it, but I don't want to risk all of my money right now."

You come up with a plan. On a warm Friday afternoon, you stroll over to the ice cream guy and say, "Hey, pal, I'd like to buy your stand, but I don't have all the money right now. How about I give you $500 to take that sign down and give me six months to come up with the cash to buy the stand at the price you're selling it at today. If I buy the stand, you can keep the $500, too. If I decide not to buy the stand, you can keep my $500, but the only catch is that you have to agree to give me the first right to buy it over the next six months; you can't sell it to anyone else, even if they offer you a higher price."

The ice cream guy looks at you, looks at his ice cream stand, looks at you, and says, "Sure, you got it."

What you've done is created an option contract. You've paid for the right to buy something at a specified price, by a specified time, but really, you don't have to buy it at all. If the neighborhood stays nice, you can buy the stand in six months at today's price. If your instincts prove true and the neighborhood goes to pot, you can walk away. Yes, you lose $500, but that's the cost of having the opportunity to buy the stand with a locked-in price that no one else can touch.

Option contracts are exactly the same. Buyers of options buy the right to buy (or short) a stock at a specified price until a specified time in the future. Sellers (otherwise known as writers) of options obligate themselves to offer the stock at a certain price, by a certain time in the future. Because they are taking the risk of being locked into the contract, they are charging you a premium for giving you the time to hedge against risk between now and when the contract expires.

Here's the twist: Before an option expires, it trades like a stock, meaning that once you buy an option, you can also sell it before the expiration date. Like a stock, you buy the option on the offer and sell it on the bid if you choose to hold the option until expiration and it is in the money. On the Monday following expiration, all of the stock automatically shows up in your account. Assume that you want the right to buy Microsoft for $50 a share six months from now, even though you think it will be trading at $60 a share. Right now—in January—the stock is trading at $45 a share. You want to buy 1,000 shares of the stock. If you were to commit to buying the full 1,000 shares now, you would have to invest $45,000, and there's no guarantee that the stock will go up anyway.

However, assume that there's an option seller (writer) out there who is willing to take on the risk of being obligated to hand the stock over to you in six months at $50 a share, rain or shine. He's obviously going to want some premium for the risk. Thus, he's willing to sell you a six-month option to buy the stock at $50, for $1 per share. Options trade in lots of 100, so to have the right to buy the whole 1,000 shares, you will have to pay him $1,000. (Each option contract is 100 shares at $1 each to buy. Thus 100 × 10 = 1,000 shares total.) You would have to buy 10 contracts to total 1,000 shares. He's charging $1 per call, so you would have to pay $100 for the right to buy each 100-share lot. Obviously, though, he's selling the options in the first place because he doesn't think the stock is going up above $50 a share. If in six months the stock isn't above $50 a share, he keeps the $1,000 and you get nothing.

There's another twist to the story, though: time. The further out the option contract is from expiration, the more he is likely to charge you for the right to buy the stock. After all, more time means more risk he has to take on, given that the greater the duration of time to expiration, the greater the chance the stock could rise above $50, which is known as the strike price.

What's more, every day that the expiration grows closer and the stock is not near the strike price of the option, he is going to decrease the value of the option, as he is an accountant, too. He knows that if the option is going to expire worthless, he is going to have to write down the option until expiration, adding a little bit of the premium decay over to the income column in his book. When an option loses value prior to expiration because it is not in the money, the event is knows as time decay. However, if the stock suddenly moved above the strike price before expiration, he would have to add the premium back in and then some more, too, to compensate for the amount of money the stock price is above the strike price.

It's important to note that you won't always make money if an option is "in the money", as the time value and intrinsic value of the option may be more than what you paid. For example, the intrinsic value of an option is today's underlying stock price, less the strike of the option. For example, assume JUN XYB 32 is a call option that you've recently purchased, whereby the stock is now trading at $35 a share. In the above example, you would have purchased the option because you thought the stock was about to move above $32 a share. And it did, as the underlying equity is now trading at $35 a share. Thus, the intrinsic value is $35 − $32 = $3. But let's assume you actually paid $4 for the option. The "time value" of the option is $1, as the $1 is the "risk premium" placed on top of the intrinsic value by the option writer, for taking on the risk. In reality, though the option has $3 of intrinsic value, the time premium added on means you're actually $1 in the hole still. Thus, it's important to note that when buying an option outright (called naked buying), you must be sure the underlying stock will move beyond the intrinsic value and the time value.

Option valuation itself, including premium and time decay, is an extremely complicated subject within itself, with many books written on it over the years. If you would like to read more about this complex subject, we strongly recommend Natenberg's *Option Pricing and Volatility*. Virtually every single options floor trader has not only read Natenberg's book but considers it the bible of options trading.

With a basic understanding of what options are, in this book we cover conceptually how traders can use various options and option strategies to profit from short-term movements within the market.

PUTS AND CALLS

Puts and calls are the actual vehicles by which options work. When you buy a call, it means you believe the stock is going up. Conversely, if you buy a put, you probably believe the stock is going down. When you buy a call, you are paying a premium, or a price for the right to buy the stock at a specified time in the future. What's more, options expire monthly, on the third Saturday of each month. What this means is that the third Friday of every month is the last trading day for the options that expire that month. Options that are not in the money expire worthless. Options that are in the money, convert—meaning that the stock is transferred from the seller's (writer's) account into the buyer's account on the following Monday morning.

In terms of notation, options are quoted as: MAR 08 XYZ $30.

The notation means that the option will expire in March 2008 at $30 a share. The XYZ is the company.

Options are quoted in an option chain, which shows the actual options—with each month of each year—for both puts and calls, side by side. Figure 13.1 shows an actual options chain.

We're not going to cover too much more about the basics of options here, as we're working on the trading concepts behind swing trading, not option theory and valuation. Next we compare normal options versus LEAP options.

LEAP OPTIONS

LEAP stands for long-term equity anticipation and basically means that the option is much like a regular option except that the time frame to expiration is longer than one year. Moreover, the buyer of a LEAP option has

Options
Ge

View By Expiration: May 08 | **Jun 08** | Jul 08 | Oct 08 | Jan 09 | Jan 10

CALL OPTIONS						Expire at close Fri, Jun 20, 2008	
Strike	Symbol	Last	Chg	Bid	Ask	Vol	Open Int
20.00	IPFD.X	6.07	0.00	5.60	6.00	3	1
22.50	IPFX.X	3.30	0.00	3.20	3.50	12	13
25.00	IPFE.X	1.35	↓0.25	1.40	1.50	10	332
27.50	IPFY.X	0.35	↓0.12	0.35	0.45	14	2,443
30.00	IPFF.X	0.10	0.00	0.05	0.15	13	332
32.50	IPFZ.X	0.08	0.00	N/A	0.05	0	20

PUT OPTIONS						Expire at close Fri, Jun 20, 2008	
Strike	Symbol	Last	Chg	Bid	Ask	Vol	Open Int
22.50	IPRX.X	0.20	0.00	0.15	0.25	100	206
25.00	IPRE.X	0.85	↑0.20	0.75	0.85	10	981
27.50	IPRY.X	2.25	↑0.30	2.20	2.30	10	171
30.00	IPRF.X	4.60	0.00	4.30	4.70	2	195

Highlighted options are in-the-money.

FIGURE 13.1 Options Chain
Source: Yahoo.com

the right to exercise the option prior to expiration, should the price of the underlying stock move in the money.

LEAP options are very risky because the sellers of the options generally demand hefty premiums for taking on long-term risk. However, when LEAP options are used correctly, they can be incredibly lucrative for the buyer.

LEAP options are great vehicles for swing traders because they mitigate some of the time decay that short-term options often hold. See, the closer an option is to expiration, while not being in the money, the quicker the value of the option drops. What this means is that the buyer of the option is losing the premium that was paid for the right to buy or sell the stock.

With this in mind, just lock away the concept of LEAP options in your head over the next few chapters. As we move through discussions about ETFs and broader market momentum, keep thinking about options and long-term options, LEAPs.

CHAPTER 14

Strategy 10: Piggyback Strategy Using ETFs and Mutual Funds

M any times in life, even the greatest minds of our time used the help of others as they went on to do great things of their own. That is exactly what we are striving to do with the ETF piggyback strategy. Even Thomas Alva Edison, whom many credit with inventing the lightbulb, had help. In fact, he did not invent the lightbulb, but rather used a 70-year-old discovery by English chemist Humphry Davy to modernize the lightbulb and created the carbon filament that burned for up to 40 hours. In trading, we are not trying to reinvent the wheel, just piggyback off the information already available.

The premise of the piggyback is to use the large-dollar research of the major financial firms to come up with new and fresh swing trading ideas. When the large financial firms build an ETF, the first step is to take an index of stocks that they feel will outperform the market. The ETF is then based on this index, and as the basket of stocks within this index moves, so does the price of the ETF. If the large firms are spending millions on research to decide which index they will base their ETF on, why not piggyback and save ourselves a few million?

The first step is to analyze which ETFs are outperforming at the current time by simply looking at performance over the past three or six months. This allows you to learn where big money is flowing and which ETFs have buying momentum behind them. After the list is accomplished, the trader should look over the top performers and choose a few areas worth trading. No more than five ETFs should be chosen as candidates because the next few steps tend to take more time.

To help you comprehend the next step, we use a real example: the top-performing ETF through the first nine months of 2007, the Market Vectors Steel ETF (SLX). As the overall market was struggling to hold onto gains, SLX was up over 70 percent. The sector clearly had momentum on its side, and traders looking for swing trade ideas on the long side often use that as a reason to buy.

Now that we have decided on an ETF that meets our criteria, the next step is analyzing the top 10 holdings of the ETF. The best place to find the information is on the specific ETF's web site, in this case www.vaneck.com. If you have trouble with the ETF's web site, www.etfconnect.com is a great source for information on ETFs and closed-end funds. The top three holdings just happen to be high-flying, international steel stocks that make for great swing trading: Rio Tinto (RTP), Vale (RIO), and Arcelor Mittal (MT). What makes this strategy great for swing traders is that it often generates fresh ideas. With thousands of potential stocks to choose from every day, the piggyback strategy allows traders to choose from stocks that clearly have buying momentum. In addition, the strategy identifies stock ideas such as the three international steel stocks that may not be household names to the average trader.

FINDING INTERNATIONAL SWING TRADE IDEAS

Because we are now in a global stock market, more and more international stocks are listed on American exchanges and are readily available for swing traders to trade. ETFs can be utilized to find stocks for swing trading ideas that are based outside the United States. One way of doing so entails using the ETF piggyback strategy with either single-country ETFs or regional ETFs. The single-country ETFs invest 100 percent of their assets in one country. An example is the iShares MSCI Mexico ETF (EWW), an ETF that invests only in companies that are headquartered in Mexico. A regional ETF covers several countries within a concentrated area. The iShares S&P Latin America 40 ETF (ILF) invests in Brazil, Mexico, and Chile. Obviously, all three countries are in Latin America, and the ETF can choose to put its money into any of the countries in that region.

The first step in finding international stocks for swing trading begins with picking the region or specific country. We'll continue to use Latin America as our example. Latin America has shown relative strength during both rallies and sell-offs over the past five years. The fundamental factors behind the region include above-average growth and stable governments, compared with other emerging markets. We will take a look at both the iShares MSCI Mexico ETF and the iShares S&P Latin America 40 ETF to give you an idea of how many swing trading ideas can be generated with one simple concept.

The first ETF to be analyzed is the Latin American ETF ILF (Figure 14.1). The top holdings will be familiar to many investors.

Number one is Vale (RIO), a large mining company based in Brazil, that has great fundamentals and based on the chart (see Figure 14.2) is a great trading candidate.

The second holding is America Movil (AMX), a large mobile phone operator based in Mexico that has operations throughout Latin America (Figure 14.3). Again, AMX has strong fundamentals and touches on one of our favorite long-term themes: emerging markets wireless communications.

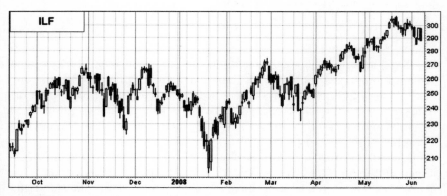

FIGURE 14.1 iShares S&P Latin America 40 ETF (ILF)
Source: Chart courtesy of StockCharts.com

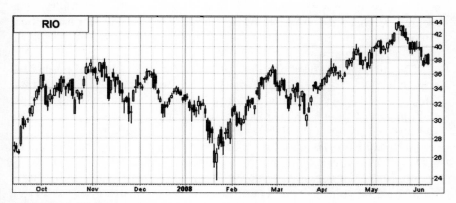

FIGURE 14.2 Vale (RIO)
Source: Chart courtesy of StockCharts.com

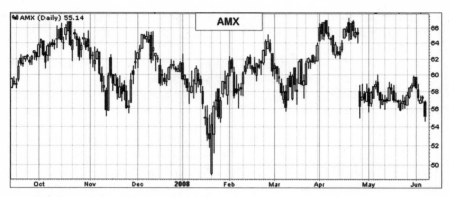

FIGURE 14.3   America Movil (AMX)
Source: Chart courtesy of StockCharts.com

When emerging markets begin to expand their telecom infrastructure, the first thought is not to lay wire across the country, but rather a wireless approach. Companies such as AMX that have a strong presence in emerging markets could be long-term winners that offer plenty of trading opportunities along the way. Just a side note: I have been to Mexico a few times recently, and everyone I see has a mobile phone device, regardless of how poor they otherwise look.

The number three holding is a Brazilian oil company that is one of the largest in the world, Petrobras (PBR). Brazil is an interesting country because it offers the rewards of the emerging markets and at the same time more stability than its peers. Petrobras has the advantage of being based in one of our favorite countries and in an industry (oil and gas) that has been great for swing traders. The daily movement in energy commodities has greatly increased the volatility of the oil and gas stocks and turned them into a trader's dream. In Figure 14.4, the chart of PBR shows the long-term uptrend and recent trading possibilities.

The number five holding in ILF is Banco Itau (ITU), one of the largest private banks in Brazil. We just discussed the benefits of Brazil and its stability. There is also the growth aspect that must be funded by someone, and once more people make more money, they have to put it somewhere. The banking sector of Brazil should benefit on both ends, and ITU has been one of the winners. I would not typically recommend an international banking stock for swing traders, but in this situation you can see that there are several trading opportunities in a short period of time (Figure 14.5).

If I asked you to name five Mexican stocks that trade in the United States, the possibility of your naming even two would be slim. To help you out, we'll piggyback the ETF industry and use their research to find

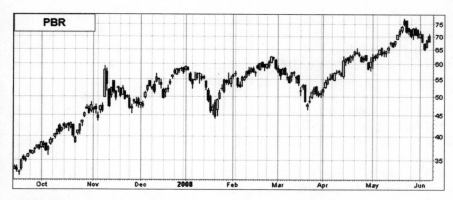

FIGURE 14.4   Petrobras (PBR)
Source: Chart courtesy of StockCharts.com

possible trading ideas south of the border. During the first quarter of 2008, the S&P 500 fell 10 percent, the worst quarter for stocks in five years. Meanwhile, in Mexico things were not that bad, and as a matter of fact, the iShares MSCI Mexico ETF (EWW) gained over 5 percent.

As traders, we can look at this divergence in two ways. First, we can look to Mexico for long ideas when we feel the trend is about to begin moving higher in the United States. The logic behind the idea is that if the Mexican stocks do well when the United States and most other countries are struggling, imagine how well they'll do when the global markets begin a new uptrend. The second idea is to use the Mexican stocks as a hedge against short positions you may have in the United States. The hedging strategy involves going short U.S. stocks because the current downtrend

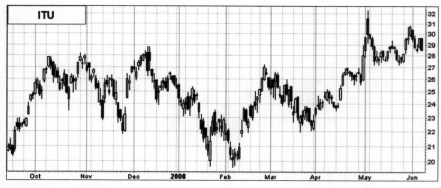

FIGURE 14.5   Banco Itau (ITU)
Source: Chart courtesy of StockCharts.com

is lower, but at the same time going long Mexican stocks. The pair trade would have worked in the first quarter of 2008, and the trends have yet to change. Not only will it give traders the ability to make money on both sides of the trade, but it also hedges against a rally in the U.S. markets that could cause a short squeeze and big losses to the short positions.

Assuming the average swing trader does not have intensive knowledge of Mexican stocks that trade here in the United States, we turn to EWW and the ETF piggyback strategy. The number one holding is a stock that has already been identified with the piggyback strategy on ILF, America Movil. Another telecom that falls in the top 10 is Telefonos de Mexico (TMX). As you can see in Figure 14.6, the stock trades in a similar fashion to AMX and has plenty of opportunities for traders to swing in and out with profits.

The last stock we will touch on in EWW is Fomento Economico Mexicano (FMX), a brewer and distributor of nonalcoholic beverages in Mexico and Latin America. A consumer staple stock is typically not the type we would consider swing trading, but the chart in Figure 14.7 shows the volatility in the stock and the swing trading opportunities.

After we've analyzed the two Latin American ETFs and named a few stocks that could be potential trading candidates, it should be clear why traders need to look outside the borders of the United States. The traders who refuse to consider international stocks are only hurting themselves because with the United States in the mature stages of the business cycle, the real growth and volatility traders must have is now overseas. Along with volatility, the international stocks also give investors the ability to create some pretty unique hedging strategies in combining U.S. and non-U.S. stocks into a pair trade.

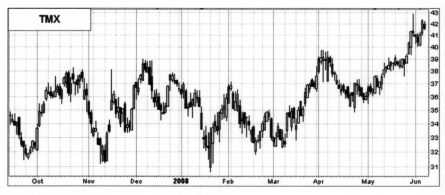

FIGURE 14.6   Telefonos de Mexico (TMX)
Source: Chart courtesy of StockCharts.com

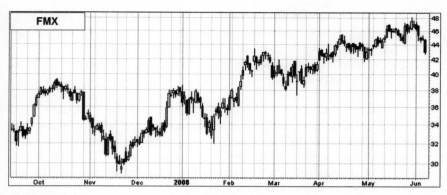

FIGURE 14.7 Fomento Economico Mexicano (FMX)
Source: Chart courtesy of StockCharts.com

PIGGYBACKING MUTUAL FUNDS

As you have probably picked up by now, mutual funds are not our favorite investment vehicle for traders or investors. Considering that fewer than 20 percent of all mutual funds beat their passive benchmark over long time periods, why would an investor choose a mutual fund over an ETF? I have no idea why investors shy away from ETFs in favor of mutual funds. If your failure rate in anything in life is 80 percent and you choose to take that route, you'd better be able to accept heartache.

Because the average investor will struggle when deciding which of the thousands of mutual funds will fall into the 20 percent category, the best route is to leave the picking to the experts and stick with ETFs. But the world of mutual funds is not a total waste. Similar to the piggyback strategy implemented with ETFs, we can also ride the coattails of the fund managers who fall into the 20 percent. There are a lot of great minds on Wall Street who make money on a regular basis, and we want access to their ideas.

The first step is to determine which mutual funds fall into the 20 percent of outperformers. To make this simple, investors can go to www.morningstar.com or finance.yahoo.com and search for mutual funds that have beaten their benchmarks over 3-year, 5-year, and 10-year periods. By using all three, we should eliminate a fund that did well only for a short period of time and that inflated the returns. Not all mutual funds have been around for 10 years, and if that is the case with one of the funds you are analyzing, simply replace the 10-year period with a 1-year period.

An asset class that often produces big stock winners that are in the midst of growing into one of the big guys is the mid-cap growth class.

Therefore, we'll concentrate on the top-performing mid-cap growth actively managed mutual funds. By using the finance page of Yahoo, we narrowed the search down to 16 mutual funds that meet our performance criteria. From there, we decided to go with the Alger Small-Cap and Mid-Cap Growth Fund (ALMAX). The fund began trading in May 2002 and has consistently beat its benchmark.

Because mutual funds do not update their holdings on a daily basis like an ETF, the transparency is not the greatest. The Yahoo web site lists the top 10 holdings of the Alger fund as of 12/31/07, which is not too bad. Granted, the holdings may no longer be in the mutual fund, but it does not matter for swing traders. If you were an investor, the attitude toward the piggyback strategy would be much different.

The top holding is FTI Consulting (FCN), a consulting firm that deals with forensic accounting and other related services. The stock is not the ideal swing trade candidate, but it does have a great uptrend and could be added to the watchlist for a buying opportunity during the next pullback. In Figure 14.8, you can see there have been opportunities on the chart to buy on pullbacks for a quick pop.

The second holding is more our speed. Bucyrus International (BUCY) has more daily volatility to trade. The stock is involved in farm and construction machinery, an area that has become a traders' playground as commodities prices soar. The chart in Figure 14.9 shows a long-term uptrend with a few big pullbacks along the way. This stock is one that can be a play on the short side when overbought levels are hit, but more likely it will be a buy candidate on all pullbacks to support.

The number four holding is Ansys (ANSS), a computer software and services company. This is another example of a stock in a long-term

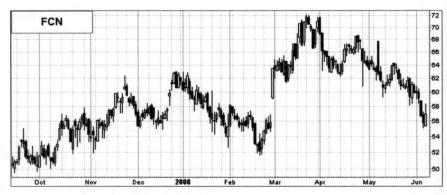

FIGURE 14.8   FTI Consulting (FCN)
Source: Chart courtesy of StockCharts.com

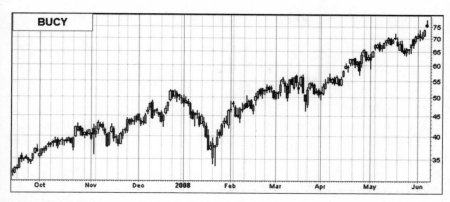

FIGURE 14.9 Bucyrus International (BUCY)
Source: Chart courtesy of StockCharts.com

uptrend that gives swing traders opportunities for easy money on pullbacks to support. In Figure 14.10, the stock pulls back to the 200-day moving average several times in 2008, only to bounce several points each time. An astute swing trader could have played ANSS several times in a three-month span.

The sixth largest holding in the mutual fund is Solera Holdings (SLH). The company is a niche software company that most traders have never heard of before. That is a shame because, as you can see in Figure 14.11, the stock has been rocking since it went public in May 2007, with lots of volatility. This stock is a great example of how a swing trader can find a new idea that can be used over and over by simply taking time to implement the piggyback strategy.

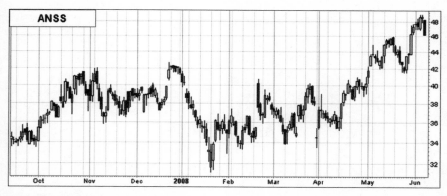

FIGURE 14.10 Ansys (ANSS)
Source: Chart courtesy of StockCharts.com

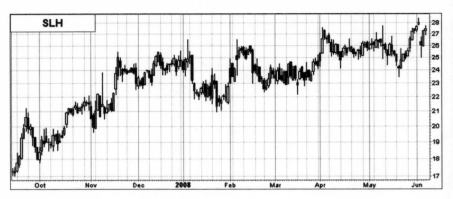

FIGURE 14.11   Solera Holdings (SLH)
Source: Chart courtesy of StockCharts.com

The beauty of the piggyback strategy is that it does not involve large amounts of time for the trader and it can be done free of charge by anyone with half a brain. Not all mutual funds will generate new ideas for you, but it is worth your time when you find a gem like SLH!

Throughout this book, we strive to present strategies that average swing traders can utilize to increase their profits. The piggyback is one of the simplest yet most effective strategies you will ever come across. Chapter 15 focuses on using scans to identify high-potential winners on both the long and short sides of the market. We will take you through the process of building and eventually running the scans that will generate new swing trade ideas.

Strategy 11: Scanning for Swing Trade Ideas

W hen the alarm goes off at 5 A.M. and the work day begins, there are 4.5 hours until the stock market opens in the United States and not a minute to waste. First things first, hit the gym for some exercise to prepare mentally and physically for the upcoming trading session. After a healthy breakfast and shower, it's time to head into the office for a few hours of premarket analysis. Naturally, the first thing a trader should do is get up to speed on what is moving the futures before the opening bell. Oftentimes merger news is released very early, along with earnings announcements. And in recent years, as the stock market has gone global, the news from Asia and Europe has become more prevalent and can often have a major effect on the movement of the U.S. market.

The news that happened while you caught some shut-eye affects not only the market but also individual stocks. If you are swing trading, you must be aware of any scheduled announcements that may affect the stocks you are currently holding in your portfolio. If you initiate a trade a day before earnings, there is a great chance the stock will either rally or sell off, depending on the number released and the reaction from other traders. If you are not staying up to date with your current positions, you are not giving 100 percent to your trading, and in the end your results will be damaged.

The news from day to day will change, and we must always be ready for the unexpected. However, there are certain tasks we can count on daily. One of the most important assignments you will have before the opening bell rings is building your watchlist for the day. With thousands of stocks and ETFs to choose from, there must be a method to the madness, or you will end up with too many or not enough ideas for the day.

One of the best and simplest ways to find trading ideas on a daily basis is scanning. Scanning uses certain criteria to narrow the number of stocks in the universe to a manageable number. The criteria are determined by the trader and are nearly limitless on most trading systems. As a matter of fact, if the system does not have the criteria you are searching for, there is a good chance it can be built by someone with the right knowledge.

ESTABLISHING A DAILY SCAN LIST

The process of using scans to find new stock ideas can be time-consuming in the beginning, but once scans are established, the rewards are reaped. Of the scans you build, only a few will stand the test of time and become one of the staples of your trading strategy. Once a handful of scans have been tested and determined to be appropriate for swing trading, they will be the first place to look for ideas each morning.

If a scan can regularly generate winning stock ideas for you, there is no reason to change. Ride the trend of the scan as long as it continues to work. Keep in mind that most scans will not always work because of the overall market environment. In a bear market, a scan to find long ideas is not the best choice for swing traders. When the markets are hitting new highs, a breakout scan will work because it rides the momentum of the overall environment. As you become more accustomed to the idea of using scans, knowing when to use each one will become second nature.

There are a number of scans that we find work well in most market environments. In the next few pages, you will be introduced to the scans in detail. The criteria are in the section that details what was used to determine the stocks that are generated by the scan. The purpose of the scan highlights why a trader would want to use the scan for a personal trading strategy. The how-to-use section breaks down how traders should take the stocks generated from the scans and turn them into winning trades.

Breakout Scan

The breakout scan is probably the favorite of most traders who are looking for a momentum play. The premise of the breakout scan is in the name; it scans the universe for stocks that are breaking out to new highs. Often, stocks that are hitting highs attract money from traders who want to ride the wave of the breakout. This is why stocks that break out continue higher for a few days before pulling back on profit taking. The goal is to catch the stock as soon as it breaks out and before the mass media get wind of it and push it high.

- Criteria
  - Average volume of at least 100,000 shares traded daily
  - Money stream (three-month range) in the top 50 percent of the universe of stocks
  - Breakout formula: ((High of the past 20 trading sessions − Low of the past 20 trading sessions) / High of the past 20 trading sessions + Low of the past 20 trading sessions) / 2 < .15 *and* The most recent close > High of the past 20 trading sessions
- Purpose: The breakout scan helps to identify stocks hitting new 20-day highs that also have a strong money stream number over the past three months.
- How to use: There are two strategies that traders can take with the breakout scan. The first is a momentum trade that looks to capitalize on the stock breaking out and involves riding the breakout for a few days. The reason a stock typically continues to rally for a few days after a breakout is the attention it garners from other traders running scans, as well as the media pushing stocks hitting new highs. Also take into consideration that traders feel more comfortable buying a stock when it is up versus waiting for a pullback. All these reasons create a buying frenzy as traders believe they must get in now before the stock runs another 10 percent. They also have a warped belief that the stock will never pull back again and if they do not buy today, the trade will be lost forever. Whatever the end reason may be, the bottom line is that stocks tend to rally for a few days after a breakout, making the stock a sitting duck for an astute and disciplined swing trader.

To make money on the breakout with the momentum strategy, the key is catching the breakout the day it occurs and using a tight stop loss order. If the one-day breakout turns into a false breakout (also referred to as a head fake), a tight stop loss allows the trader to quickly exit the trade with a minimal loss. The one situation you do not want is holding onto a stock that failed to continue the breakout and the next day is back below the breakout level. This is a very negative situation and could even be considered a shorting opportunity for the quick-witted trader.

Because scans are often computed after the close or before the market opens, the stock is included in the breakout scan only if it closes above its previous 20-session high. This eliminates the intraday false breakout that may occur (see Figure 15.1).

Traders should consider the situation with the market the day after the stock makes the breakout scan list. If the futures are pointing to a down day, it may be best to hold off on buying. On the other hand, a strong open to the market is likely to spur more buying momentum in the stocks that

FIGURE 15.1   Failed Breakout Known as a Head Fake
Source: Chart courtesy of StockCharts.com

broke out a day earlier. Before placing the buy order for the swing trade, the trader must have an entry zone that highlights the price willing to be paid for the stock. If the stock gaps open higher by more than 3 percent, it should not be bought because you do not want to chase the action. There will always be another opportunity around the corner; never settle for a trade just because you want to trade. On the down side, if the stock gaps lower, it may be back below the breakout point, which will also nullify the trade idea.

The second price that must be established is the stop loss. Typically, it will be approximately 1 to 2 percent below the breakout level (see Figure 15.2).

FIGURE 15.2   Stop Loss on the Breakout Scan
Source: Chart courtesy of StockCharts.com

Placing a buy order in the opening minutes will initiate your new swing trade, and with the stop loss already calculated, it becomes a wait-and-see situation. After breaking out, a stock may run for a few days or a few hours before the momentum swings back into the direction of the bears. This causes the trader to be diligent, and when the momentum begins to wane, it will be time to take the profit and run. That being said, it is important to not get an itchy trigger finger and sell too quickly. A 2 percent trailing stop loss is a good gauge to use after the stock begins to move higher after the purchase (see Figure 15.3).

Overbought Scan

Most traders would rather pay more for a stock and buy it when it is up versus waiting for a pullback and improving the reward-to-risk setup. The overbought scan attempts to identify stocks that have strong money flow and are in intermediate-term uptrends, but at the same time off their highs according to the RSI reading. In an ideal situation, traders will be able to identify stocks that are uptrends and buy them during their normal pullbacks. Remember that even the strongest uptrend will have a series of higher pullbacks that can be referred to as higher lows. The goal of this scan is to identify stocks that have big money flowing in and at the same time have an RSI reading under 50, suggesting the stock is pulling back from a high or rallying off a higher low.

- Criteria
  - Average volume of at least 100,000 shares traded daily
  - Money stream (three-month range) in the top 25 percent of the universe of stocks

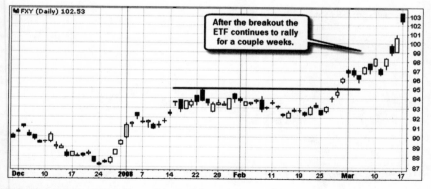

FIGURE 15.3 FXY Rallies after Breaking Out
Source: Chart courtesy of StockCharts.com

- Money stream (one-year range) in the top 25 percent of the universe of stocks
    - Relative strength index (RSI) below 50
- Purpose: The oversold scan will find stocks that have pulled back from their highs and at the same time still have strong money stream readings.
- How to use: The oversold scan can be used in all market environments and therefore is a versatile tool for swing traders. When the market is in an uptrend, the scan helps identify strong stocks that are experiencing healthy pullbacks. This allows the trader to buy a stock with an attractive reward-to-risk setup and limits the downside risk. When the market is in a downtrend, the scan identifies stocks that are off the highs and at the same time have a strong money stream, which is rare in a down market. The combination should make for stocks that have a high probability of rallying in the near term. When the market is trendless, which is more often than you think, the scan finds stocks that are at the lower end of their trading range and are considered buy candidates that should rally to the upper end of the trading range (see Figure 15.4).

Volume Surge

One of the single best indicators to determine what is happening internally with a stock is volume. When the volume increases dramatically, it signals that someone knows something we do not know or at least someone is making a very large bet in one direction or the other. A dramatic volume surge could be caused by a mutual fund dumping a large number of shares,

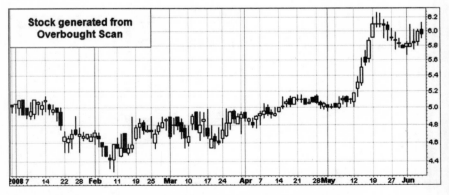

FIGURE 15.4 Example of Stock Generated from Overbought Scan
Source: Chart courtesy of StockCharts.com

thus pushing the daily volume well above the norm. If Mutual Fund A decides it must sell a large amount of XYZ stock, it may not mean much to the average trader. However, it does have a ripple effect across the industry that will set off another series of events.

Let's think about this logically. If Mutual Fund A begins selling its shares of stock XYZ, that's a red flag to Mutual Fund B and Mutual Fund C. The managers at the latter are concerned about beating their benchmarks each year, but more important, want to at least keep up with their competitors. If Mutual Fund A sells the shares of stock XYZ and the stock continues to fall, it could create a situation of underperformance for Mutual Funds B and C. So what must Mutual Funds B and C do to protect themselves against that type of situation? Sell. That is why a volume surge on the downside often leads to lower prices in the coming weeks.

The same situation happens when a volume surge occurs on the upside. If Mutual Fund A is buying shares of a stock, its competitors are likely to get in on the act in the near future. The volume will also attract individual buyers and traders who are seeking increased liquidity (see Figure 15.5).

- Criteria
  - Average volume of at least 100,000 shares traded daily
  - Top 5 percent in five-day volume surge

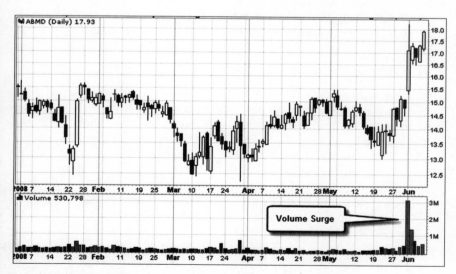

FIGURE 15.5 Example of Stock Generated from Volume Surge Scan
Source: Chart courtesy of StockCharts.com

- Additional criteria can be added if the scan concentrates on either the short side or the long side.
- Purpose: The scan identifies stocks that have a surge in volume over the past five trading sessions. When there is big volume, there is more to the story, and often a big move is ahead. As swing traders, finding the next big mover is important.
- How to use: What makes the volume surge scan different is that the stocks highlighted do not have a typical pattern they follow. For example, the breakout scan will be made up of stocks that have bullish chart patterns hitting new 20-day highs. The bare-bones volume scan does not discriminate against strong or weak patterns, and that leaves the door open to a variety of stocks for the list.

The trader must take some time to look through the stocks to find which patterns, whether bullish or bearish, are appropriate for their trading strategy. To simplify things, traders can sort the stocks in the scan by an overbought/oversold oscillator, depending on their end goal. Another option is to add more criteria to the scan to eliminate stocks that are not going to meet the objective of the scan. For example, if the trader is searching for stocks that are buy candidates, eliminating all stocks that are over 10 percent from the high would be a possible criterion. This would result in stocks with volume surges near a high. The probable outcome is stocks that are surging toward a new high, but keep in mind that the scan is not perfect, and a stock that is falling on heavy volume from a high could also be in the mix. This is why I will reiterate that scanning is just one facet of the trading strategy; the ability to read charts is also integral.

High Short Interest Ratio

The focus of the high short interest ratio scan is pretty obvious: the short interest ratio (SIR). For traders who need a quick refresher on the short interest ratio, according to Investopedia.com, it is a sentiment indicator that is derived by dividing the short interest by the average daily volume for a stock. This indicator is used by both fundamental and technical traders to identify the prevailing sentiment the market has for a specific stock.[1]

Short Interest Ratio = Short Interest/Average Daily Trading Volume

The end result is a number that is always above 0 and can be as high as 25 when a stock has a large number of shares short. Some traders look simply at the short interest of a stock, which is the actual number of shares short. This is helpful, but unless the number is compared with the average volume of the stock, it is meaningless for our purposes. For example, stock

XYZ has 4 million shares short, and stock ABC has 2 million shares short. At first glance, you would assume that stock XYZ is more heavily shorted. In theory, there are more shares short at this time, but how does it compare with trading of the stock? Stock XYZ trades 2 million shares per day, and therefore the short interest ratio is 2.0. Stock ABC trades only 250,000 shares per day, and the short interest ratio is a higher 8.0. This is why I often cringe when someone is discussing the number of shares of a stock that are short versus the short interest ratio.

The short interest ratio is important because it tells us a lot about the underlying internals of the stock. A high short interest ratio suggests a large number of traders are betting the stock will move lower in the weeks and months ahead. A low short interest ratio is often found on stocks that have solid long-term charts and those that have a low beta and make small moves from day to day. Traders who play the short side of the market are often successful at what they do and can be considered aggressive, with the type of personality that leads them to enjoy living on the edge. If you think about it, over the long term the stock market moves higher, so in theory the short sellers are fighting the long-term trend of the market. That is why short sell trades often are swing trades, unless there is something fundamentally wrong with the stock.

Finding a stock with a high short interest ratio is great, but that is only half the story. The next question traders must ask themselves is "What type of trend is this stock currently in?" When a stock is in an uptrend and the short interest ratio is high, the majority of the time it indicates traders are trying to pick the top. They feel the stock is overbought in the short term, are therefore looking for a pullback, and would like to profit from any impending move lower. This is a very risky way to make a living because, as I like to say, "The trend is your friend until it ends." Picking bottoms and tops is a risky proposition, which unless properly understood, will result in losses. Please also see Chapter 11 for more information. That type of countertrend trading will put you in the poorhouse very quickly.

The short interest ratio scan searches for stocks with a high ratio that are near a high. More on the specifics of the scan will come later.

If the stock traded in a downtrend and the short interest was high, it probably indicates the short sellers have already made money and are now riding the trend lower for bigger profits. If you want to hop on the short train, it is not a bad trade, but to short with the traders that are already on the short side. The one thing you must remember is that when the stock begins to give an indication that the downtrend is slowing or coming to an end, it will result in a large number of short sellers running to the buy counter along with the bulls who are already there. Basically, it could cause a short squeeze, the price could explode very quickly, and a winner may now become a loser.

- Criteria
    - Average volume of at least 100,000 shares traded daily
    - Short interest ratio above 8.0
    - Price per share above $10
    - Trading within 5 percent of the 90-day high
    - Falls in the top 25 percent of one-year relative strength versus the S&P 500
- Purpose: To find stocks trading near their 90-day highs and have a high short interest ratio (above 8.0). Stocks in this situation have a high probability of a short squeeze if they are able to hit a new high and the short sellers are forced to sell. This creates a run to the buy side, and the stock explodes higher.
- How to use: The high short interest ratio scan is best used in a bull market when breakouts are occurring on a regular basis. Ideally, the scan should identify stocks that are trading just below a 90-day high on the way up or stocks that have recently pulled back from hitting a high and are within 5 percent of the recent high-water mark.

The reason this scan works well is because short sellers are typically smart traders who know that it is key to take small losses and move on to the next trade. Therefore, when a stock breaks out to a new high, the short seller was wrong and will cover the position, thus creating a short squeeze and a sizable rally for the stock. Because we want to go with the trend of the market, which in this case is higher, our strategy is to take the other side of that trade and buy in anticipation of the breakout and eventual short squeeze (see Figure 15.6).

FIGURE 15.6 A Stock Generated from High Short Interest Scan
Source: Chart courtesy of StockCharts.com

CHAPTER 16

Strategy 12: Swing Trading a Market Sell-Off

Over the long term, the stock market has always moved higher. As a matter of fact, I challenge you to find any 20-year period when the Dow did not move higher. That being said, why would any long-term investor want to fight the trend of the market and implement a shorting strategy?

The key word is *long-term*. For investors with a time horizon that goes out a few years for their investments, going against the long-term uptrend of the market is a flawed strategy. Because this book concentrates on swing trading, however, it is important to note that traders play the short-term and intermediate-term trend, whether it is up or down. There may be periods when the market moves lower for months at a time, and swing traders must use a shorting strategy to make money.

Even the strongest bull markets experience pullbacks as investors digest the rally and bank some profits. For example, entering the summer of 2006, the U.S. indices were in the fourth year of a strong bull market that began off the lows in 2002. During the summer of 2006, the Dow fell 8 percent from the May high to the June low. When the market corrects, it often takes down the majority of stocks. During the summer 2006 correction, 87% percent of the components of the S&P 500 lost ground. Even more interesting is that over half fell more than the index. Therefore, most traders that were buying lost money during the pullback.

I know swing traders who will only go long and look to buy stocks in both up and down markets. During an uptrend, this makes perfect sense; however, during an intermediate-term downtrend, your odds of buying a stock and making money fall dramatically. In every situation, the key is to

find the best reward-to-risk opportunity; in a down market, the best opportunities are on the short side of the trade. Therefore, we will dedicate this
chapter to swing trade strategies that can help you profit when the market
is falling.

SHORTING STOCKS: PROFIT WHEN THE MARKET IS FALLING

Before moving onto specific shorting strategies, we'll explain in depth the
process of shorting a stock. In general, when an investor sells short a stock,
the goal is to profit from the fall in the price of that specific stock. Most
beginning investors get very confused when they realize it is possible to
make money when a stock falls in price. In actuality, selling stocks short
is not complicated at all, and once you get the hang of it, it is as easy as
buying a stock.

Troubles with Shorting

The biggest argument the naysayers have against a short sell strategy is
that the potential loss is infinity. Theoretically, that argument is true, but I
have yet to find a stock that has gone to infinity. If a strict risk management
plan is in place for the position, the losses should be the same as they
would be for a long position. When a trader buys a stock, the lowest it
can fall is zero, and the maximum dollar loss is the amount paid when the
stock was purchased. If a stock is sold short, by contrast, it could continue
moving higher forever, and the losses could pile up very fast. Keep in mind
that more than a risk management strategy will help to eliminate the upside
risk. You are likely to receive a margin call that leads to a forced sale before
the losses move to unmanageable proportions.

The other main criticism of short selling is that it is un-American.
Maybe I am way off base, but since when is making money through hard
work considered un-American? The goal is not to drive the price of the
stock down to zero and put the company out of business. As swing traders,
we are simply looking to profit from the natural up and down cycles of a
stock. There is also the belief that the long-term market trend is higher and
that anyone who shorts the market is going countertrend and thus lowering
their odds of making money. As I stated earlier, as a whole the market does
move in a long-term uptrend, but in the short term there are opportunities
to make money on pullbacks in the market cycle.

Pros of Shorting

The most obvious benefit of short selling is the ability to make money when the stock market is falling. We all know that stocks do not go up every day, and there are times when a stock gets ahead of itself and is due for a 10 percent correction. By using the knowledge you're acquiring, you'll see times when it is obvious a stock is due to fall, and now you can profit from the high-reward, low-risk setup with a short sell strategy.

One reason many swing traders love to use a short selling strategy has to do with the velocity of the moves. How often have you watched a stock go up 20 percent in three months, only to have the entire gain wiped out in one day? You are not alone. Negative news (poor earnings, downgrade, failed product launch, etc.) can bring down a stock in a matter of minutes and wipe out the gain that took months to build. Many swing traders have a propensity to search for big winners, and this brings them to the short side of the market. In Figure 16.1, CROX falls over 27 percent on the back of a negative earnings report.

Even long-term investors should read this chapter because short selling can be used as a hedging strategy during intermediate-term pullbacks. A great example occurred in late 2007, when the S&P 500 hit a new all-time high on October 11. Within three months, the index was down nearly 20 percent from the high, and many stocks suffered even bigger losses. The market remained in a long-term uptrend; however, it got hit with a flurry of negative news, and the end result was a 20 percent correction in a short period of time. The gains that took more than one year to build were gone in a matter of months (see Figure 16.2).

An investor who implemented a shorting strategy with ETFs could have lessened the damage to a portfolio with a few simple trades. We will touch on ETF hedging strategies later in this chapter.

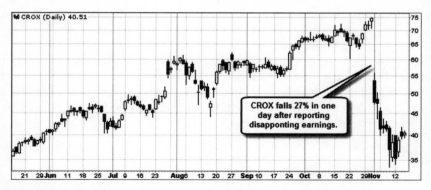

FIGURE 16.1 CROX Falling on Earnings Report
Source: Chart courtesy of StockCharts.com

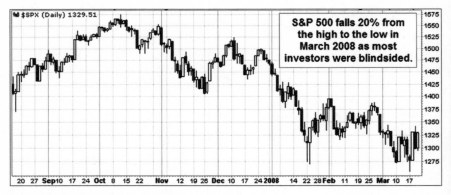

FIGURE 16.2 Correction of the S&P 500
Source: Chart courtesy of StockCharts.com

Dynamics of Shorting

An investor who sells short a stock is actually borrowing shares from the broker and selling them to another buyer. The money generated from the sale goes into the investor's account. At some point in time, the investor must buy the shares back (ideally at a lower price, and then a profit will occur).

Let's assume on October 18, 2007, you feel CROX is becoming overvalued, and at the same time the stock market is struggling to break to a new high (see Figure 16.1). Technically, the stock gave an RSI crossover sell signal, and all signs are pointing to at least a small pullback. An order to short 1,000 shares of CROX at $70 is entered, and the amount of $70,000 is placed into your account. Over the next two weeks, it appears the trade may have been placed at the wrong time, as the stock moved as high as $75, but the stop loss of 10 percent was never triggered, and the short was still in place when the stock fell 27 percent on November 1. A disappointing earnings report sent CROX tumbling, and the value of the short sell position much higher. Because most earnings mishaps last a few days, the short sell is not covered for another week at $40/share. To close out the trade, the investor must buy back the 1,000 shares that were sold short at the current market price. On November 8, a sell order at $40 is triggered, and the investor must pay $40,000 to buy the 1,000 shares.

Initial Trade	Sold Short 1,000 shares of CROX at $70/share	+$70,000
Closing Trade	Bought Back (Covered) 1,000 shares of CROX at $40/share	−$40,000
Net Profit		+$30,000

When the trade is looked at in the example, it can be more clearly understood. In reality, the investor paid $40 per share and sold it at $70 per share, thus resulting in a profit of $30 per share. For a moment, assume the investor bought the stock at $40 and sold it at $70; the same profit would have been achieved. The goal of buying a stock is to sell it at a higher price in the future. When shorting a stock, the goal is to sell it at a higher price; the one difference is that the selling takes place first.

INTRODUCING SHORT ETFs

In 2006, as the universe of ETFs began to expand rapidly, one of the more exciting introductions involved short ETFs. A short ETF returns the inverse of the index it is linked to. For example, the ProShares Short Dow 30 ETF (DOG) will return the inverse of the Dow Jones Industrial Average on a daily basis. If the Dow falls 1 percent, DOG rises 1 percent, and vice versa. Short ETFs are also referred to as inverse ETFs or bear ETFs.

Over the past few years, the number of short ETFs has risen dramatically. They now not only cover the major indices such as the Dow and S&P 500 but also focus on specific sectors, such as utilities and technology. In addition to the expansion into sectors, a number of ETF companies have rolled out leveraged short ETFs. A leveraged short ETF does exactly what the name says: It gives a trader leverage without the use of margin. The ProShares UltraShort Dow 30 ETF (DXD) rises 2 percent on a day when the Dow falls 1 percent.

Table 16.1 is very interesting for one specific reason. All but two of the ETFs on the list fall into the leveraged short or short category. As we

TABLE 16.1   Most Actively Traded Short, Ultrashort, and Leveraged ETFs

ETF	Symbol
ProShares UltraShort QQQ ETF	QID
ProShares UltraShort S&P 500 ETF	SDS
ProShares UltraShort Russell 2000 ETF	TWM
ProShares Ultra QQQ ETF	QLD
ProShares UltraShort Dow 30 ETF	DXD
ProShares Ultra S&P 500 ETF	SSO
ProShares UltraShort Financials ETF	SKF
ProShares UltraShort Oil & Gas ETF	DUG
ProShares UltraShort Real Estate ETF	SRS
ProShares UltraShort Mid-Cap 400 ETF	MZZ

mentioned, traders have a tendency to prefer taking the short side of the trade because stocks tend to fall faster than they rise. The list backs up that statement in a strong way. Granted, the U.S. stock market was in the midst of a sell-off at that time; however, the overwhelming amount of shares traded in short ETFs cannot be ignored.

Using Short ETFs as a Trading Vehicle

Over the past year, as the volatility of the market increased and the major indices went into correction mode, the popularity of the short ETFs as trading vehicles rose substantially. A perfect example is the ProShares UltraShort Financials ETF (SKF). In October 2007, the average daily volume for the ETF was approximately 825,000 shares per day. By the end of March 2008, the average daily volume for SKF hit 9 million shares per day. I have to assume a large portion of the volume came from short-term traders and hedge funds making short-term bets that the financial sector would continue to fall (see Figure 16.3).

Before the introduction of short and ultrashort ETFs, traders had to rely on actually short selling stocks to take advantage of market drops. In the situation with SKF, an investor would have had to either short an individual financial stock or short an ETF that is concentrated on the finance sector. Because many traders look at selling short in a different manner and for some reason do not react the same way to the trade, the short ETFs are a great product.

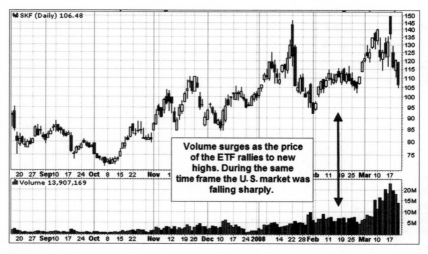

FIGURE 16.3   Volume Surge of SKF
Source: Chart courtesy of StockCharts.com

Not only do the short ETFs open up a new world to traders who use typical brokerage accounts but also they create new opportunities for retirement monies. Due to investment restrictions, traders are not allowed to sell short stocks or ETFs in their retirement accounts (IRA, Roth IRA, IRA Rollover, 401K, etc.). Older traders who have been taking advantage of the tax-sheltered accounts over the years often have very large sums of money in IRAs. In the past, if the market was dropping, the trader either had to try to go against the trend and buy or else move into cash or fixed income. Expect to see more activity in the short and leveraged ETFs in the future as traders attempt to play every change in market trends.

With traders finally realizing the trading possibilities outside the United States, there are new products that take advantage of the global market swings. One country that garners the most attention, both good and bad, is China. The Shanghai Index in China rose nearly 100 percent in 2007 and was up fivefold in a matter of two years. When a stock market surges in a parabolic manner, it is not uncommon for the sell-offs to be violent. In the first three months of 2008, the Shanghai Index was down 34 percent.

Until November 2007, traders who wanted to play the fall of China had the option of shorting Chinese stocks that are traded on U.S. stock exchanges. The ProShares family of ETFs introduced the UltraShort FTSE/Xinhua China 25 ETF (FXP). In the first month of trading, the ETF averaged a move of 7.6 percent per day. On the third day of trading (November 12), the ETF gained 13.5 percent. The following day FXP fell 16.3 percent. If this is not a trader's dream, I do not know what is. Figure 16.4 is a six-month chart of FXP that shows the volatility possible for swing traders.

FIGURE 16.4 Daily Volatility of FXP
Source: Chart courtesy of StockCharts.com

Aside from swing traders using the short ETFs to play very short-term swings that can be lucrative and damaging, they can be used to trade intermediate-term themes. The short trade of the financial stocks during the U.S. credit crisis that began in 2007 was a major theme that could have been exploited with the UltraShort Financial ETF (SKF) (see Figure 16.3).

Besides the obvious themes that are hitting the headlines of the newspaper, there are other trends that can be profitable for short-selling traders. For example, an ETF I recommended for subscribers to my newsletter, the *ETF Bulletin*, was the ProShares UltraShort Consumer Services ETF (SCC). As the credit crunch was beginning, the housing market was starting to tumble, and consumers were not spending as much. The logical sector to get hurt by a slowing economy and a weakening consumer is retailers and consumer services. This is why I turned to SCC as a trading vehicle on July 31 as the stock market was in the midst of a sell-off. The ETF was sold with a 12 percent gain a few weeks later (see Figure 16.5).

Overall, the short and ultrashort ETFs are a great trading vehicle for swing traders who would like exposure to the short side of the market and have an appetite for volatility. When trading the ETFs, I suggest you look for either short-term technical setups or intermediate-term themes that could move the ETFs. Just as with any trade, make sure you have a stop loss in place to protect against wild swings.

Using Short ETFs in a Hedging Strategy

Market timing is a large part of becoming a successful swing trader. The key is that you must be correct about 50 percent of the time to be profitable. This is the case because if you implement an appropriate profit

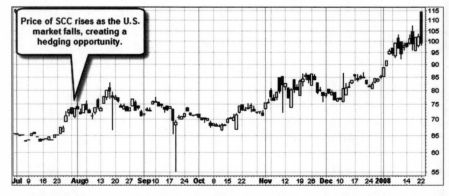

FIGURE 16.5 Using SCC to Hedge against the Slumping Housing Market
Source: Chart courtesy of StockCharts.com

management and risk management strategy, the result will be big profits and small losses.

Long-term investors do not put market timing at the top of their list because it would require a lot of time and effort that in the long run may hurt the performance of the portfolio. Considering most long-term investors do not have the knowledge of timing the market and make their decisions based solely on emotions, they should leave the market timing to the professionals and traders.

But before we move away from the market timing topic, there is a small piece of this strategy that could be useful for long-term investors. As we have mentioned time and time again, the stock market does not go straight up or, for that matter, straight down. So why not hedge our portfolio during times when the market is in the midst of a correction to protect our portfolio performance?

Long-term investors typically hold the stocks they buy for an average of a few years and within that time ride the market ups and downs. There are only two ways for investors to protect their overall portfolio during a market correction. They could sell most of their holdings to lower their exposure to the market, or they could hedge their positions with short ETFs.

We will begin with an example before breaking down the process even further. Assume an investor has a $100,000 portfolio composed of 75 percent stocks and 25 percent money market. The forecast for the market in the coming months is not good, but the investor may not want to sell his stocks for tax purposes or because they are considered solid long-term investments. Whatever the reason may be, the investor would like to protect the portfolio from a correction in the market, which will directly affect the performance of the individual positions.

If the stock market were to pullback 10 percent over the next two months, the portfolio would fall 7.5 percent, assuming the 75 percent in equities falls the same amount as the market. This is not bad because the portfolio outperformed the overall market. But the investor would like to do better and take advantage of the fact that there are short ETFs available.

If the investor decides to put the 25 percent in the money market into a short ETF, the end result would be a loss of 5 percent. The portfolio would have an allocation of 75 percent long and 25 percent short, a net of 50 percent long.

If the investor feels very adamant about the impending correction, a leveraged short ETF could be purchased with the 25 percent. The portfolio would now have an allocation of 75 percent long and 50 percent short, a net of 25 percent long. The end result would improve to a loss of only 2.5 percent.

The differences may not appear to be very drastic, and all three strategies still result in a loss at the end of the correction. Sure, you can look at the glass half empty, or half full. In reality, the portfolio is better poised for the next market rally and will not only be starting at a higher level than it would have without the hedge, but now every percentage move higher results in a larger gain.

To better accentuate the point we are getting across, assume there are two investors. One begins with $100,000 and the other with $150,000. They both make 20 percent in the market over the next 12 months. The first investor will make $20,000 and have an ending balance of $120,000. The second investor will gain $30,000 and now have a balance of $180,000. The difference between the two accounts has risen by $10,000 to $60,000 because the starting balance of the second investor was larger. The amazing benefits of compound interest will allow the second investor to continue increasing the size of the difference over the years.

The example should help you understand why it is important not only to make money when the market moves higher but also to preserve capital when the market falls. As a matter of fact, the most successful investors and traders are those who are able to outperform the benchmarks when the market is in the midst of a sell-off.

Downside to Using Short ETFs

Unfortunately, nobody has yet to find a strategy that guarantees outstanding performance without risk to the downside. The number one risk with the hedging strategy is that investors may be too early or too late to the game. For example, assume an investor believes the market is due for a pullback and implements strategy number 3 (see Table 16.2). But in the end the market rallies another 5 percent, and the portfolio gains only 1.25 percent and lags the overall market by 3.75 percent. It is not the worst thing that could happen because the investor still makes money at the end of the day, but less than the benchmark. The investors need to ask themselves if they are willing to lower their potential reward on the upside for a limited downside exposure. In essence, using short ETFs for hedging is similar to buying insurance. It limits your potential loss.

TABLE 16.2   Results of Three Hedging Strategies Using Short ETFs

Strategy	Equities	Money Market	Short ETF	Leveraged Short ETF	Return
1	75%	25%	-	-	−7.5%
2	75%	-	25%	-	−5.0%
3	75%	-	-	25%	−2.5%
Market	100%	-	-	-	−10.0%

When trading the ultrashort ETFs, the trader must realize that the 2-to-1 leverage is based on the daily returns. For example, if the NASDAQ 100 rallies 2 percent in one day, the ProShares UltraShort QQQ ETF (QID) should fall by 4 percent in theory. The next day the NASDAQ falls 1 percent and ends up with a two-day gain of 0.98 percent. The ETF will rally 2 percent the second day and end with a two-day loss of 2.08 percent. The loss of QID is more than double that of the NASDAQ 100, and thus the tracking error begins. Granted, the two-day difference is only 12 basis points (0.12 percent), but over time this number will grow and could eat into profits very quickly. This is why the ultrashort or ultralong ETFs should be reserved for short-term swing trading or hedging. Any other type of investment strategy will result in subpar results that are combined with above-average risk.

CHAPTER 17

Strategy 13: Swing Trading the Megatrends

W e must first begin with the definition of a megatrend. The first step is to break down the word: *mega* is a synonym for large, and *trend* describes the general direction of the market or stock. Therefore, a megatrend is can be defined as a large, long-term direction within the market. In the 1990s, a new megatrend developed; today we know this trend as the Internet. The entire Internet sector moved higher for a decade before the Internet bubble burst in 2000. Our goal is to help you find the megatrends that are currently available to investors and the next potential megatrends that are on the horizon. At the same time we want you to realize that even megatrends do end at some point and you cannot buy and ignore.

Traders may be wondering why megatrends are important to swing trading—and this is a great question. Oftentimes the megatrends last for a decade, as the Internet megatrend did in the 1990s. We do not expect you to transform yourself from a swing trader to a long-term investor, but that does not mean that the megatrend strategy cannot work in your favor.

WHY TRADE A MEGATREND?

If Figure 17.1 does not give you chills down your spine, then you are not meant to be a trader. The chart of the Internet Index in the late twentieth century shows how a megatrend can make all passengers onboard large amounts of money. Whether you are a swing trader, a day trader, or an old buy-and-hold investor, one of the keys to success is going with the overall

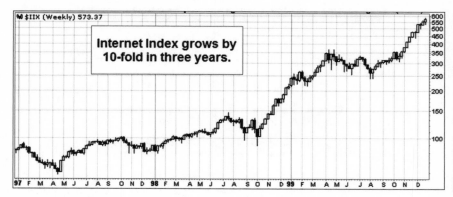

FIGURE 17.1 Internet Index—Interactive Weekly (1997–1999)
Source: Chart courtesy of StockCharts.com

trend of the market. When it comes to the megatrends, we feel you will be able to increase the probability of your trading success by going with the long-term uptrend. In the world of swing trading, the more chips that are stacked in your favor, the better the odds of picking a winning trade. What better place to start than with a long-term megatrend that, if we are right, will result in higher prices for years to come. As the old adage says, "The trend is your friend until it ends."

It is clear why a trader would have been on the long side of the Internet trade from 1997 through 1999. In that two-year time frame, the Internet Index rose nearly five times, and many of the individual stocks did even better. Take Microsoft (MSFT), for example; the stock rose from a low of $9 in the beginning of 1997 and got as high as $51 by the end of 1999. Then there is Yahoo (YHOO), which rallied from less than $1 to a high of $108 in 1999!

As the daily chart of Yahoo in Figure 17.2 shows, the stock is clearly in an uptrend that could have the term *rocket ship* attached to it. That being said, there are numerous pullbacks along the way that could have been considered buying opportunities to swing traders who were watching the Internet stocks.

Investors must realize that with approximately 6,000 stocks traded on the three major exchanges, it is nearly impossible to take advantage of every buy and sell opportunity. This is where the megatrend strategy becomes integral to the success of a swing trader. By identifying one or two megatrends, a swing trader will be able to focus on all stocks that fall into the category. If you were tracking the Internet stocks, there is no doubt in my mind that one of the stocks on your watchlist would have been Yahoo. In the end, identifying a megatrend will help a trader narrow the number of stocks on the watchlist and free up more time to make money.

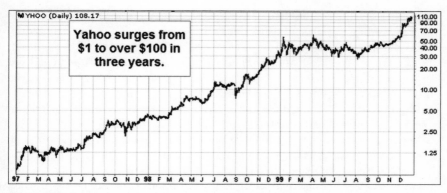

FIGURE 17.2 Example of Megatrend: Chart of Yahoo!
Source: Chart courtesy of StockCharts.com

If you look at any long-term megatrend, whether it is the Internet rally of the 1990s or the housing rally from the mid-1990s to 2005, all have ups and downs along the way. But the overriding similar factor is the ability to rally to new highs after each pullback. As swing traders, we will have a great opportunity if we can take advantage of the pullbacks and buy into the weakness in anticipation of the trend continuing.

From the chart of Yahoo, it is clear the stock pulls back every few months and in essence is offering alert swing traders an amazing buy opportunity. From April through June 1998, the stock moved sideways and drifted lower after hitting a high in early April. When this occurs, the impatient trader would lose interest in the stock. However, the disciplined swing trader realizes the stock is simply consolidating and experiencing a healthy pullback. Instead of taking Yahoo off the watchlist, the trader will put it to the top of the list and wait for the stock to begin moving higher for confirmation the pullback is over. A buy signal should be generated as the stock moves off the lows. In the two months after the pullback, Yahoo doubled in price, giving investors a large window of opportunity to make sizable profits.

HOW TO TRADE A MEGATREND

Trends are important in swing trading because if you are not going with the trend, the probability of picking a winning trade decreases dramatically. Have you ever tried to short an uptrend? Or better yet, attempt to swing trade to the long side as the stock market is falling? Unless you are one of the best traders ever or you are extremely lucky, my guess is that you lost money in both situations.

Because a megatrend will last several years, swing traders will have numerous trading opportunities throughout the long-term uptrend. If you decided to play the megatrend from the perspective of an investor, the strategy will differ from that of a swing trader. The long-term investor will look for a reasonable entry price based on the overall market and the specific megatrend and, when the time is right, begin accumulating shares of related stocks and ETFs. On the other side of the fence is the swing trader, who has a much shorter time frame and will look to utilize one of the two swing trading strategies that are perfect for playing megatrends: buying on the pullback and riding the wave of momentum.

Of the two strategies, the easiest one to play is riding the wave of momentum (RTWM) because it is more comfortable for traders to buy a stock when it is hitting highs or moving higher that day versus buying a stock that has been lower for several days. This is based purely on human emotion because, in theory, buying on the pullback (BOP) is a much better strategy. Think about it logically. Most stocks do not fall for more than three days in a row, and the same can be said about a rally, that stocks rarely move higher every day of the week. So in theory, if you are buying a stock after three down days, the probability of picking a short-term winner should be higher. Unfortunately, we have yet to complete this study in full; however, after years of trading, I can bet the numbers will favor the BOP strategy in the short term.

The true reason a swing trader prefers the *momentum* trade is because in their hearts they want to be a day trader who can make money from minute to minute. If you are trading for a few pennies, it makes perfect sense to ride the momentum of the stock that is moving higher. But if you are truly a swing trader and looking to catch the intermediate swings, you have the option of waiting for a pullback and increasing your odds.

Buying on the Pullback

The BOP strategy offers one of the better reward-to-risk setups because it allows the trader to buy close to support, thus lowering the potential risk and at the same time increasing the reward. Take a minute and think about what I just said: The BOP strategy can lower risk and increase reward at the same time. No, you have not died and gone to heaven, but you sure did find a great strategy that most traders are too scared to implement.

To help you visualize the benefits of playing the BOP strategy, there are two charts of the biotech company Illumina. The first chart (Figure 17.3) shows Illumina one week after gapping to a new high in January 2008. The stock pulled back five consecutive sessions, and from a swing trader's perspective, the setup was close to a BOP setup. But before buying, we must determine where the support level lies. As you have learned about

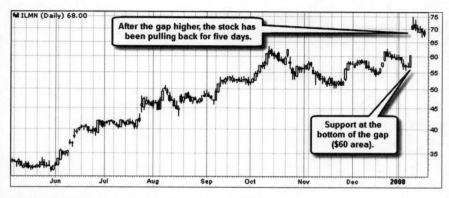

FIGURE 17.3 Determining Entry on a Pullback
Source: Chart courtesy of StockCharts.com

gaps, the bottom of the gap, which in this case is $60, is strong support, and more often than not, the gap is filled before the next rally begins. Therefore, the support is at the $60 area. A swing trader buying at $67 cannot have a $7 stop; that would equate to over 10 percent risk. That being said, I am sure there were swing traders who felt that the stock had pulled back enough and went ahead and bought with a stop of a few dollars. Let's find out who was right: the trader who could not wait or the patient swing trader.

In the second Illumina chart (Figure 17.4), you see that the impatient trader would have been stopped out with a loss in the position. However, the patient investor had an opportunity to buy $1 above the gap and feel comfortable about doing it because the stop-loss was only $2 below the

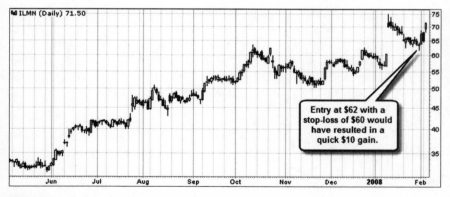

FIGURE 17.4 Importance of Patience during a Pullback
Source: Chart courtesy of StockCharts.com

entry price of $62. Three days later, the stock was up $10, and I am sure the patient swing trader did not get greedy and banked a sizable profit. Well in actuality most traders are greedy and need to take a gift when they receive it.

To bring the importance of reward-to-risk home even more, let's look at just the numbers. The impatient swing trader would have bought Illumina at $67 and would have had to put a stop loss of $60 if the chart was being used. The upside would have been the intraday high set a week earlier at $75. The reward was $8 and the risk was $7. The reward-to-risk ratio was 8-to-7.

The patient swing trader waited for Illumina to get closer to the bottom of the gap that is often filled. The entry price was $62, and the stop loss was $60. The target was the same, $75. The reward-to-risk ratio for the patient trader was 13-to-2. You do not have to be Einstein to figure out which trader will be more successful over the years. Notice how when you wait for a pullback to support that not only does the risk shrink but also the reward increases. Go tell your friends you found a way to lower risk and increase reward, and they will either think you are crazy or will love you. Either way, you will become a more successful swing trader, now that you understand this concept.

Getting back to the megatrend theme, it is time to take a look at a megatrend that is currently underway—rising energy prices. The price of oil went from $20 per barrel in 2003 to $110 in early 2008. There are many winners and losers with oil trading above $100 and gaining more than 400 percent in five years. We will not fight the trend and therefore look to make money playing the upward swings in the stocks that benefit from rising oil prices. Figure 17.5 is a chart of Exxon Mobil, the largest oil company in

FIGURE 17.5 Playing the Energy Megatrend with Exxon Mobil
Source: Chart courtesy of StockCharts.com

the world and currently the largest overall company in the United States. Naturally, higher oil prices help their bottom line, and the weekly chart reflects the uptrend during the past three years.

The beauty about playing Exxon and the rising energy price megatrend is that both the long-term investor and the swing trader can walk away with their pockets full of money. A long-term investor could have bought Exxon at $30 in 2003 and tripled her money in five years. At the same time, a swing trader had more than enough opportunities to buy Exxon on a pullback in anticipation of a rally.

Riding the Wave of Momentum (RTWM)

Everything said about the RTWM strategy so far has had a negative tone, so you are probably wondering why it is even being discussed. Even though there are some downsides to the strategy, when used correctly, it can be a great way to make quick money through swing trading. When a stock has momentum and is in the middle of a megatrend, it is not unusual for big moves in a short time.

The commodity megatrend, which began in the early 2000s, includes a monumental rise in the price of gold bullion. There have been periods of momentum, followed by stagnation, and once again momentum. Figure 17.6 is a chart of the exchange-traded fund that tracks the price of gold futures. The SPDR Gold Shares ETF (GLD) has been in a long-term uptrend since it began trading in late 2004, but throughout the majority of 2007, the ETF was moving sideways between $62 and $67. That is, until the price of gold and the related ETF broke out to new highs in early September. From early September through early November, there were no sizable pullbacks,

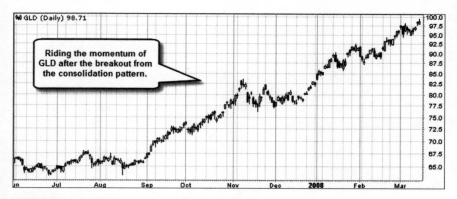

FIGURE 17.6   Riding the Momentum with GLD
Source: Chart courtesy of StockCharts.com

and a swing trader could have easily placed a trailing stop loss and let the trade run from $67 to $83 (Figure 17.6). This would be a pure momentum trade that resulted in big gains in a short period.

CURRENT MEGATRENDS

Water

The one commodity that everybody overlooks is one of the most abundant resources on planet Earth—*water*. Even though water can be found in most places on the globe, a very small portion of it is drinkable. According to the World Health Organization, less than 1 percent of the world's freshwater, or 0.007 percent of all the water on Earth, is readily available for human consumption. If you find that that statistic amazing, how about the fact that 1.1 billion people live without clean drinking water. And even more, 2.6 billion people, lack adequate sanitation. Nearly 2 million people around the world die each year from diarrhea diseases. All the numbers come from a credible source, the World Water Council.

The reason the price of oil has been surging this decade is in large part from the demand for the black gold from emerging countries. Ten years ago, the demand from China, India, and other emerging countries was nowhere near the levels of today. As the emerging countries prosper, it creates more wealth for the nation, which should eventually trickle down to the citizens.

This movement of the money into the hands of the population is creating a major phenomenon in countries like China and India—the emergence of a middle class. Until now, there have been the haves and the have-nots. But with the have-nots able to make money in the booming economy, there is now a middle class that is willing to spend money and demands the necessities of life, such as clean water and adequate sanitation. This population and wealth growth creates the need for more clean water and the infrastructure to make it possible.

In the emerging countries, the water megatrend will focus on supplying clean water to people who do not have the luxury of access to safe drinking water. To achieve this, there must be a very expensive buildup of infrastructure to supply the clean water and also systems in place to find available clean water. It might be from drilling wells or by taking water from the ocean and using desalinization plants. Either way, hundreds of billions, if not trillions, will be spent on helping the entire world gain access to safe drinking water and sanitation.

In the developed countries, we do not have the same water issues as those in the emerging countries, but it does not mean there are no problems for us. Even though I pay for my bottled water every day, little do I know that the water system beneath me is deteriorating. Many of the pipes that run under our major cities, especially in the Northeast, have been in place for decades (in some cases centuries!) and are in dire need of replacement. According to the United Nations, $1.5 trillion will be spent on water infrastructure over the next 10 years. The EPA says the U.S. water systems need hundreds of billions of dollars in upgrades and repairs. The agency went on to say that water will eventually be the single largest expenditure in the entire U.S. economy.

When the word *trillions* is being tossed around, I tend to listen. And being a believer in the water megatrend for a few years, I have no doubt in my mind that money can be made by investing in related stocks in the coming years. That being said, there will be ups and downs along the way, and that is where swing traders can take advantage of the pullbacks and momentum plays.

Commodities

The subprime issue that rocked Wall Street at the end of 2007 and has carried over into 2008 can be credited with crushing the financial stocks and taking down the majority of the stock market. One of the few areas that was able to sidestep the selling was the commodities. As demand for goods continues to increase worldwide and the supplies dwindle, there will be more upside for investors putting their money to work in the current commodities megatrend.

There are three distinct groups within the commodity megatrend that are available for investors: energy (oil, natural gas, etc.), metals (gold, copper, etc.), and agriculture (wheat, corn, etc.). All three areas saw their share of new record highs during the first quarter of 2008 as investors viewed the area as not only a safe haven during rough times but also a supply-demand investment. When the demand for food rises because of a growing middle class around the globe and the supply of wheat and corn is falling due to weather issues and ethanol use, there is only one way prices can go—up.

I can make a similar case for the energy commodities and metal commodities. Another factor in the three areas is the fall of the U.S. dollar. As the greenback falls, it makes commodities, which are hedges against inflation, more attractive. Since 2002, the U.S. dollar has been in a free fall, and there appears to be no end in sight.

Swing traders can play the commodities megatrend with two different strategies. The first would be to trade the stocks that are related to the sector, such as gold-mining stocks or oil and gas production companies. The choices are enormous if that is your strategy. The second option would be a newly introduced investment vehicle, the commodity ETFs. Instead of having to open a futures account to trade the price of the commodity futures, there are now ETFs that track the futures price of commodities such as gold, silver, oil, natural gas, and copper. The charts can be studied in the same manner as stocks, and oftentimes technical analysis works even better for the futures.

Infrastructure

The double-digit growth in China requires more office buildings, roads, power grids, grocery stores, and so on. This booming buildup in China and other emerging markets requires one key element—infrastructure. The great infrastructure megatrend might begin in China and India, but it ends in the United States. The United States has one of the oldest and most inadequate infrastructure systems in the world, and it is one of the richest nations on the planet.

When it comes to government spending, the money always makes its way to areas that are not considered priorities, but within the past year it has become clear the United States has made their infrastructure system a major priority. After the steam pipe explosion in Manhattan and the deadly bridge collapse in Minnesota, the government stepped up efforts to begin funding an infrastructure rebuild across the nation. The water infrastructure mentioned earlier is just one aspect of this megatrend. There is also the transportation sector (bridges, highways, trains, subways, etc.), power transmission (see: New York blackout), and office buildings for the growing population.

Sectors in the infrastructure megatrend that swing traders need to be made aware of are heavy construction, building materials, cement, lumber, construction machinery, and engineering. The stocks that make up these sectors have been movers and shakers the past few years, and we expect more good things to come in the future. Keep in mind that the big movers also have big pullbacks, and that is when swing traders should be champing at the bit to make their move and ride the new uptrend for a week or two.

Brazil, Russia, India, China (BRIC)

The four most recognizable and popular of the emerging markets are the BRIC countries: Brazil, Russia, India, and China. Not only are they four of the largest emerging countries in the world but also they have four of the fastest growing economies. When investors are searching for growth in their portfolios, they can no longer look at the United States as a whole. The GDP growth in the United States will probably remain in the 3 percent to 5 percent range. On the other hand, the BRIC countries will have GDP readings close to double digits for the rest of the decade and offer investors the only true consistent growth.

A study by Goldman Sachs ventured that only the United States and Japan will have larger economies than the BRIC countries by 2050. I realize that is a long way off, but the point I am trying to get across is the megatrend that can be played by swing traders in the future. Think back on the United States and how in the early twentieth century, it was a booming economy in the midst of the industrial revolution. The opportunities were endless, with steel companies and car companies rising with parabolic moves. The same types of rallies have occurred and will continue for the BRIC stocks. As swing traders, we will have a large number of stocks and ETFs to choose from in our trading. Also, most BRIC-related investments carry a high level of volatility with them, a factor that can generate a lot of trading opportunities.

THE NEXT MAJOR MEGATREND

The Next Frontier: Africa

Ten years ago, the thought of investing in China and Brazil would have brought laughter from most traders. Today, China and Brazil are two of the hottest countries in the investment world, and their stock markets are up several times over in that time frame, much better than that of the U.S. stock market. It is not too late to put money into the BRIC countries, as you have just read, but getting in 10 years ago would have made a serious difference to your bottom line, and the compound interest effect is out of this world.

Most of the countries in the world have moved to the status of at least emerging market, but nearly an entire continent remains behind the times—Africa. Sans South Africa, the majority of the continent is still very much a third world county at best. That being said, huge strides have been made over the past decade, as investment money realized the opportunity in the continent.

China, one of the fastest growing countries in the world, has taken a liking to Africa and has quickly become one of the continent's favorite trading partners. According to the Xinhua press, the trade between China and Africa reached $55 billion in 2006. This compares to less than $10 million a generation earlier.[1] The same study shows that 750,000 Chinese immigrants now call Africa home, in search of economic riches.

There are two major reasons Africa has the potential to be the next China for traders and investors: the abundance of natural resources on the continent (oil and minerals) and the backing of the developed world.

The commodity stocks have quickly become great trading vehicles for swing traders as big money has found its way into the alternative asset classes. The increased liquidity has led to higher volatility and thus new opportunities for swing traders to profit. The growth around the world has led to an increased demand for commodities ranging from oil to copper, and the abundance of untapped natural resources available in Africa can lead in only one direction.

Not only are Africans beginning to believe in the entrepreneurial way of life but also the developed nations around the world see opportunity in the continent. Everyone from China to the United States has been investing money in start-ups and moving operations to Africa to be the first to tap into the unlimited riches. When multibillion-dollar companies are battling to be the first into a new area, it can only mean one thing—more money to be made.

As swing traders, we do not have too many options today when it comes to trading the African market. However, I believe there will be more African-based companies moving their listings to the United States to help raise capital for future growth. The favorite play of many swing traders that has exposure to Africa as well as other emerging markets is Millicom International Cellular. The company is a wireless telecom play that has a large presence throughout Africa and could have a major role in expanding communications in the continent. More opportunities similar to Millicom will become available in the coming years, and as an astute swing trader, you must be ready to take advantage of them.

CHAPTER 18

Strategy 14: Return on Assets and Return on Equity

W e've covered many swing trading strategies thus far, and we still have some ground to cover on options. Before then, we need to discuss the balance sheet, income statement, return on assets (ROA), and return on equity (ROE) here to give traders just a little more fundamental confirmation for attempting to seek trades. Fundamental valuation can help find great longer-term plays, something that we can capitalize on with options, specifically LEAP options.

Moreover, return on assets and return on equity, when used from a trader's perspective, can be rock-solid secondary confirmation for another swing trade strategy or, when used alone, can also prompt us on potentially overvalued and undervalued fundamental situations. From a trader's perspective, we don't really have hours and hours to dedicate to mind-numbing research; rather, when looking at financials, we need to be there and gone fairly quickly. With this in mind, we will leave the never-ending fundamental research to the analysts. For our purposes, though, we'll take a little time to understand what's happening within a company's balance sheet and income statement, while also allowing ROA and ROE to help our research.

BALANCE SHEET AND INCOME STATEMENT

Balance sheets and income statements are important to us as traders, even if they're not much fun to dig through. Rather than an in-depth analysis of balance sheets and income statements, however, we'll take just a quick glimpse at each here and note a few highlights of what traders should be looking for.

Balance sheets are simply the larger bank statement of the company. Balance sheets list the assets, liabilities, and ownership equity (shareholder equity) of a company. One of the primary items listed on a balance sheet is cash. Cash is a current asset. Current assets are liquid assets that a company can use almost immediately to meet its short-term obligations. Long-term assets include property, plant and equipment, intangible assets like patents, and any other asset that does not have short-term liquidity.

Liabilities are short- and long-term debts, including accounts payable, taxes due and deferred taxes, promissory notes, and minority interests.

One of the ways traders can quickly gauge a company's short-term financial health is through the current ratio, which is current assets divided by current liabilities. If the current ratio drops below 1, the event is a distinct short signal, as we can infer the company is in trouble and can't even meet short-term liabilities. On the other hand, if a company has a current ratio of 2, a company has enough liquidity in reserve that, if all sources of revenue were shut off tomorrow, the company could pay its liabilities two times over before feeling a cash crunch.

At the end of the day, if you want to truly look at the assets a company is carrying, the balance sheet is the place to look.

The income statement is a company's quarterly and annual measure of profitability, or lack thereof. Here we can immediately find a company's revenue and also see how sales translate to net income. The income statement is important for several reasons. First, many newer growth companies have large promises and few returns. When a company is showing a strong balance sheet but a dismal income statement, unless the company is expecting a massive source of revenue in the near future, investors with common sense can infer that although the balance sheet may be strong today, without income, it's unlikely to stay strong for long.

Just a little lingo clarification, *top line* always refers to revenue (sales), and *bottom line* refers to net income (revenue less all expenses).

Within the income statement, we can derive earnings per share (EPS), which is calculated as

$$\text{Earnings Per Share} = \frac{\text{Net Income} - \text{Preferred Stock Dividends}/}{\text{Weighted Average of Common Shares Outstanding}}$$

Within EPS, we always want to look at diluted EPS, which accounts for all stock options, warrants, convertible bonds, and other securities that can eventually be converted to common stock and thus dilute earnings by adding more shares in the marketplace. Do not be confused when a company reports two sets of earnings: diluted and nondiluted.

RETURN ON ASSETS

Return on assets (ROA) is a great indicator for investors looking to learn how profitable a company is relative to its assets. Really, at the end of the day, almost all assets within a company should generally have some type of contribution to earnings, if a company is operating as efficiently as possible.

The overall calculation of ROA is fairly simple. Annual earnings are divided by the company's total assets.

$$ROA = Net\ Income/Total\ Assets$$

There are several points about ROA that traders should be aware of. First, as a general rule of thumb, the higher the ROA, the better. However, some industries have higher ROA numbers than others. For example, an industry that requires a substantial amount of capital investment in depreciating assets would probably have a lower ROA than an industry that carries little property and depreciable assets.

With this in mind, it's always a good idea to reference ROA numbers only within the same industry, so you don't derive a skewed perception by looking at an unrelated sector.

Here's an example:

Company A (an online retailer) has net income of $5 billion and assets of $5 billion.

Company B (an airline) has net income of $5 billion and assets of $10 billion.

Company A would have an ROA of 100 percent.

Company B would have an ROA of 50 percent.

Clearly, Company A is utilizing its assets better than Company B; however, Company B is in a totally different ballpark and thus cannot be compared. This reminds us that we must always look at comparable companies within the same industry to have an accurate measure that we can truly benchmark.

RETURN ON EQUITY

Return on equity (ROE) is net income divided by total equity and is a measurement of common stock against net income. In terms of ratios, ROE is viewed as the one of the most important, as it quickly shows us how much profit is generated from assets minus liabilities (total equity).

$$ROE = Net\ Income/Total\ Equity$$

What's more, ROE is also a signal of earnings growth and of the amount of money a company reinvests in its future. Some high-ROE companies aren't always the best investments, though, because in some industries, where few assets are required (think of the example in the previous section on ROA), high ROE can be misleading. Fact is, companies with high ROE but with few assets may actually prove to be incredibly risky over the long haul. When we consider that an airline must have much more capital to invest in infrastructure, we intuitively know that the ROE numbers will be lower, based on the heavy burden of assets the company must carry. However, a dot.com with virtually no assets (which shows a much higher ROE) certainly isn't necessarily a better investment, especially considering the here today, gone tomorrow paradigm behind technology companies.

What's more, when a company pays out dividends, the event takes away from ROE, something investors must be aware of. If a company has a 10 percent dividend yield, overall earnings growth is lowered, as the dividend payment takes away from earnings growth. In addition, earnings growth is lower when a company uses its income to buy back shares of stock in the open market.

So another ROE formula comes into play when you are considering dividends and buybacks. Return on common equity (ROCE) is a way to circumvent preferred dividends by simply dividing preferred dividends by common equity and then subtracting net income.

$$ROCE = Net\ Income - (Preferred\ Dividends/Common\ Equity)$$

Much like ROA, ROE is applicable only within an industry. However, when we look at various companies within a particular sector, the companies with higher ROAs and ROEs are often better bets because they indicate a much more efficient use of assets and earnings.

Swing traders will often want to take a look at a company's balance sheet, income statement, ROE, and ROA. However, short-term movements are generally not based on deeper fundamental issues, like those in this chapter. Really, the items in this chapter should serve as confirmation of a trade, though at times quick short-term trades can contradict fundamentals.

Note that expected income growth is important even when you trade on a short-term basis, especially if you're short. When a company has rock-solid expected income growth numbers (think PEG ratio), stepping in front of a moving train can be reckless, even if the stock is slightly overvalued. The simple fact of the matter is that investors can stay exuberant for long periods of times.

Stocks move on emotions, and if the market is moving a stock higher, even though the balance sheet, income statement, ROA, and ROE are not very good, then from our perspective, the market is right, not the fundamentals. More than likely, the stock will eventually correct to a point of fair valuation, but usually that takes time.

CHAPTER 19

Strategy 15: Covered Call Options

C alls are options that allow an investor the right, but not the obligation, to buy a stock at a future price. For the right, the investor must pay a price, which is known as the option premium.

Here, we'll go over a strategy that is similar to but slightly different from calls and serves to do one of two things. Covered calls, via the framework here:

- Allow an investor the opportunity to buy a stock at a discount, *or*
- Give an investor the possibility of locking in profits as a percentage, over a period of time

WHAT IS A COVERED CALL?

A covered call is different from the normal action of buying a call. Instead of buying a call, the investor is this time on the other side of the coin and selling (writing the call). Normally, writing calls is about the riskiest proposition in options trading: Should the trade go against you, the risk is substantial. Professionals usually sell options and amateurs buy them, which is why most people lose money in trading options. The guys taking on the most risk are the ones who really know what's going on. In essence, their risk is incredibly hedged, and every move is calculated. By writing covered calls, average investors are able to step into the pro's shoes, while significantly limiting risk.

When pros write options, they are expecting the options to expire absolutely worthless. The seller's risk is the price difference between the strike price and the price at which he must hand over the underlying stock, should it expire in the money. Here's an example of why writing calls naked—that is, not covered—is so risky. If you wrote calls for XYZ stock at $10 a share six months from now, and the stock rallies 100 points, and assuming you did not already own the stock, at expiration, you would have to go to the open market and buy the stock to hand over to the buyer of the option. Basically, you would have to buy the stock for $100 a share and thus lose $90 for every share that you're required to hand over. I hope that you see why writing calls naked is so dangerous and should be left to the pros.

However, when writing covered calls, you not only offer (otherwise known as sell, or write) the call but also buy the underlying stock at the same time. What this means is that if the stock ascends above the strike, you hand over the stock at expiration and lose no further cash. In fact, you would actually profit from the difference between how much the stock gained from the price at which you bought it and the strike price, plus the premium you collected in writing the calls. The limitation? Your upside potential is capped. If the stock screams upward, you do not capitalize on the movement over the strike price.

Here's an example: Joe buys 100 shares of First Solar for $200 a share. He then writes one contract (equivalent to 100 shares of the underlying stock) of the December $250 calls for $15, totaling $150 in premiums collected. Then, at expiration in December, the stock is actually trading at $280 a share. Joe profits $65 a share. The profit comes from the difference between the price he paid for it ($200) and the strike ($250), totaling $200. The extra $150 is the money he received for writing the calls. However, someone who bought the stock in the open market would have profited $80 per share from November to December, outpacing the option writer's call by $15 a share.

Given that there's the potential that option writers will clip their own profits, we might ask, "Why would they write options at all?"

The answer is that the stock may not go up at all, and if it doesn't, the option writer gets to keep the premium paid for the option that was never exercised.

Does the option writer have downside?

Yes, the option writer loses money if the stock drops below the price paid for it, less the premium received. In other words, in the First Solar case, the stock would have to decline $15 under the price the option writer purchased it for before the position was negative.

Basically, the stock would have to drop $15 before the initial investment in FSLR would move into the red. When you consider the ramifications of the latter point in this section, the overall picture of covered calls becomes very interesting. Really, we begin to see that writing covered calls gives the option writer the possibility of buying stocks at a discount.

BUYING STOCKS AT A DISCOUNT

In short, when an option expires worthless, writing the call actually allowed the writer of the call to purchase it at a 7.5 percent discount to the current market price, no matter where the stock trades, as long as at expiration it is trading under $250 a share. The 7.5 percent is calculated by taking the amount of the option premium ($15) and dividing it by the price per share of the stock ($250); the end result is 7.5 percent.

Thus, investors who would like to own a stock at a discount and think the stock will stay flat or even fall in the near term can write covered calls to lock in the stock at a price lower to market. If the stock rallies, though, and the writer has to hand over the shares, the worst-case scenario is settling with the profit collected from the options.

DEEP IN THE MONEY

There's another options strategy that is not only reliable but also quite incredible at the same time. It's a deep-in-the-money LEAP covered call option strategy. We are writing covered calls for calls that are already in the money. What we're hoping to do is simply lock in the option premium to ensure constant returns over the long haul.

Here's how it works: First, the deep-in-the-money strategy can be a little tricky to use because the setups can be hard to find. Why? The premium received has to be slightly higher than usual to compensate—on a percentage return basis—the amount of equity we will be locking up for whatever the holding time is.

Here are the nuts and bolts: Suppose stock XYZ is trading at $40 a share now (April) and you suddenly notice that the October $30 calls are trading for $15. (This is a slightly exaggerated example, by the way.) To write one contract, we would buy 100 shares of the stock at $40, putting $4,000 to work. Then we would sell (write) one contract (100 shares) of the October option for $15, thus immediately putting $1,500 in our pockets.

We're expecting the stock to be called away in October. Then, as planned, in October the stock is called away at $40. We would not gain or lose any money from giving away the stock, as we were obligated to hand it over anyway. However, we do get to keep the option premium.

The return would be calculated as the original stock price ($40) minus the premium we were given ($15) = $25, which is our cost basis. Then, we would subtract the cost basis ($25) from the strike price ($30) = $5 profit on the trade. To get our percentage return, we would then divide the profit ($5) by our cost basis ($25), which would give us a return from April to October (six months) of 20 percent. However, because we held the position for only six months, the actual annualized return (assuming we can do it repeatedly) would be 40 percent, a huge gain. What's more, we had virtually no risk in the trade.

In reality, though, large returns for deep-in-the-money covered calls average about 20 percent, on an annualized basis. Basically, when we're utilizing this strategy, we're trying to maximize a percentage return on an annual basis with little risk. You could say that this strategy is almost like bonds, except that we are not really holding debt of any type, other than the obligation we have to the buyer of the options.

In essence, we are the debt issuer and are being compensated fairly for giving the investors the ability to exercise the option in the future, while almost knowing—for certain—that our shares will be called away.

CHAPTER 20

Strategy 16: Straddles as a Profit Tool

H ere you'll read about a strategy that can help you make money with options no matter which way the market goes. This strategy will take some careful consideration, especially the risk aspects. However, the basic principle is this: When a stock, ETF, or index consolidates, it means that it travels laterally for a considerable amount of time, in other words, there is no apparent up or down trend. Seasoned traders know though, consolidation is similar to a snake coiling and getting ready to strike. However, you may not be sure where the strike will be aimed, so the straddles (and strangles, too!) are meant to help you profit no matter what the outcome. With this in mind, before we get into straddles proper, let's take a look at how to identify straddle setups.

CONSOLIDATION IS KEY

As already mentioned, consolidation is when prices begin to coil laterally (or slightly up or down), causing the trading range becoming tighter and tighter. When a stock or index coils, look out, because something is about to happen. Consolidation can occur in a truly lateral range, but more often than not, it happens in a sort of wedge. Figure 20.1 shows exactly that. During March and April of 2008, airlines experienced considerable consolidation, as the market attempted to figure out whether the stocks within the industry were bottoming out or simply setting up for a move lower.

FIGURE 20.1   AMEX Airline Index (AMEX: XAL)
Source: Chart courtesy of StockCharts.com

After a significant move downward, a market instrument consolidation is what's known as a bear flag, alluding to another move lower on the horizon. From time to time, however, the bear flag can surprise Wall Street by not being a bear flag at all. The ensuing upward move rips the rug out from underneath bears' feet, as they scramble to cover shorts. This is exactly why straddles and strangles are perfect for periods of consolidation where uncertainty looms, because they potentially give the trader a profit in either direction. Look again at Figure 20.1, which shows consolidation.

In Figure 20.1, the consolidation within the industry was indeed a bear flag, setting up for a move lower. Around mid-April, the index fell though the floor, about 23 percent before recovering later that month. Traders who were exposed only to the long side probably took a bath as airlines fell from grace yet one more time.

As another example, Figure 20.2 shows International Paper (NYSE: IP), which displayed considerable consolidation throughout all of February and half of March. With oil still on the rise and many commodity input prices also running through the roof, investors inferred slowing revenue for the company. What's more, timber-related products, on the whole, were seeing lower demand, as the slowing in housing and in building materials began taking a bite out of the bottom line.

FIGURE 20.2 International Paper First Consolidation
Source: Chart courtesy of StockCharts.com

At this point, many investors were probably considering buying International Paper, possibly wondering whether demand would begin to return for timber products, especially because the Federal Open Market Committee had been lowering interest rates, and business borrowing/spending would ensue. Still, significant danger loomed in the industry, and thus another big move down just couldn't be ruled out.

As the Figure 20.2 shows, consolidation ensued, just before a large move downward.

Both of the previous examples show two things: When consolidation occurs, a large move is often just around the corner. And second, during periods of consolidation, you will want to consider why consolidation is occurring at all. Really, consolidation is a period when investors just don't have a significant reason to buy or sell. Consolidation is when investors (and Wall Street) really aren't too sure what to expect from the future and, at the end of the day, aren't doing anything.

The large moves that occur after consolidation are probably because the market instrument has created stress within both institutional and at-home investors as they watch the stock or the index move sideways. When the market instrument breaks support or resistance, which is usually clearly defined, a wave of panic buying or selling ensues.

Now that we have a better understanding of the exact environment that is most profitable for straddles and strangles, let us look at the two strategies to see how they work with this coiling.

Straddles entail buying a put and a call option at the same time. The time and strike price make straddles slightly different than strangles.

STRADDLES

For straddles, an investor buys both a put and a call with the same price and expiration date. The straddle buyer is saying, "I don't know where the stock is going, but I'm going to create a market-neutral hedge, and to keep all things similar, I'm going to do it with the same strike price in the same month."

What the investor is sure of is that the stock price will move significantly. Without a big price movement, the investor is likely to lose money, as the winning side gains may not offset the losing side's premium-paid losses. More on this in a moment.

Here's an example on how a straddle works in real life. Looking at our second chart of International Paper (Figure 20.3), we see that in the first part of May, the stock began to consolidate again. Moreover, given

FIGURE 20.3 International Paper Second Consolidation
Source: Chart courtesy of StockCharts.com

that the past two consolidation periods were followed by significant gaps lower, investors may want to short the stock again. However, the stock is trading near a 52-week low and has seen two major slides already in 2008. Could the bottom be nearing? Obviously, there are plenty of questions as to the stock's direction, which gives us a great scenario for a straddle trade.

If we take a look at the option chain shown in Figure 20.4, we are looking at the options for June 2008. What we want to find are the lowest priced options with the closest strike price to where the stock is trading now. Why? When the option moves in our favor, we want to gain the quickest 1-to-1 price movement in the option with the stock. This is called Delta.

What we could then do is purchase the JUN 08 $25 calls for $1.35 and the JUN 08 $25 puts for 85 cents.

Here's where the trade gets risky. As soon as the options begin to move, we have to close the losing side immediately to preserve as much premium

Options

View By Expiration: May 08 | **Jun 08** | Jul 08 | Oct 08 | Jan 09 | Jan 10

CALL OPTIONS					Expire at close Fri, Jun 20, 2008		
Strike	Symbol	Last	Chg	Bid	Ask	Vol	Open Int
20.00	IPFD.X	6.07	0.00	5.60	6.00	3	1
22.50	IPFX.X	3.30	0.00	3.20	3.50	12	13
25.00	IPFE.X	1.35	↓0.25	1.40	1.50	10	332
27.50	IPFY.X	0.35	↓0.12	0.35	0.45	14	2,443
30.00	IPFF.X	0.10	0.00	0.05	0.15	13	332
32.50	IPFZ.X	0.08	0.00	N/A	0.05	0	20

PUT OPTIONS					Expire at close Fri, Jun 20, 2008		
Strike	Symbol	Last	Chg	Bid	Ask	Vol	Open Int
22.50	IPRX.X	0.20	0.00	0.15	0.25	100	206
25.00	IPRE.X	0.85	↑0.20	0.75	0.85	10	981
27.50	IPRY.X	2.25	↑0.30	2.20	2.30	10	171
30.00	IPRF.X	4.60	0.00	4.30	4.70	2	195

Highlighted options are in-the-money.

FIGURE 20.4 International Paper Options
Source: Chart courtesy of StockCharts.com

as we can. What's more, the option must move beyond the strike price, plus the premium we've paid, for both sides of our position, to be profitable.

In the case of International Paper, let's assume the stock suddenly gaps down to $25 and then slides into $24, before starting to trend back up. We'd be profitable right?

Wrong.

First, we paid 85 cents for the put option, which means the stock must trade below $24.15 before we're in the black on the put side. But don't forget that we also paid $1.35 for the call. Assuming we were able to salvage 50 percent of the call premium, we would then have to subtract the difference from the stock price, after already subtracting the premium we paid for the put. The math would look like this:

$$\$25 - \$0.85 - (\$1.35/2) = \$23.48$$

The stock would have to fall 8.5 percent from the last closing price (denoted on the chart as $25.67) before we were ever profitable. Thus, the bottom line is to trade straddles, and we had better be pretty darned sure that the stock is going to make a *huge* move. Don't forget, there are commissions to account for too.

If we look at the International Paper chart again, we see that when the stock gapped down (and slid South over the next four sessions), the total move from $32 a share equated to just about a 16 percent decline. If the stock were to fall 16 percent again, the price would end up basing around $21.57. If this happened, we would clear roughly $1.97 in profit on the option trade, denoted as our break even ($23.48) minus the profit target ($21.57) = $1.97. And considering we paid $2.20 for the straddle, our total return is $1.97/$2.20 = 89.5, or a 90 percent return. The question is, though: Do you think International Paper is going to fall another 16 percent before the expiration in June, which is just six weeks away?

Probably not.

Understanding the Risk with Straddles

By the way, when trading straddles, or strangles (the same as a straddle, but with different month expirations) on consolidation, we don't want to go out too far, as the longer the time frame, the more expensive the options. We do risk, however, rapid time decay, should the stock not move at all or only move slightly in one direction. You must know what you are doing and understand the risks of options when trading straddles or strangles.

When the market thinks that a stock is about to make a big move, it often prices in the risk of the large move in the option. As fear rises, so does volatility, and the option's price as well. What we have to understand here is that after a long period of consolidation, it may not pay to purchase a straddle, even if you are expecting a large move, because the premiums for the options may offset any gains. Traders often try to sell the losing half right after the move begins, but as those who've traded options before know, the floor is all too quick to immediately remove premiums from losing options. Why? The guys who wrote the options want to keep their premiums, and thus losing options can see speedy time decay.

With everything that we've covered here, it's important to take the time to understand that trading straddles can be very, very risky—something we never want to do blindly. What's more, we really want to take serious time when attempting to figure out how low (or high) a stock can move. One tool we've already discussed in this book that can help project movements is Andrew's pitchforks, which aid in finding profit targets, should a stock be consolidating within a trend. Because pitchforks often measure troughs and rallies (which can sometimes be denoted as straddle setup consolidation), pitchforks can easily provide great guidance to figuring out whether the risk of taking on a straddle is worth the potential profit at hand.

CHAPTER 21

Strategy 17: Bull and Bear Spreads

So far, we've covered option basics, LEAPs, covered calls, and straddles and strangles. Next are bull and bear spreads, which are excellent options tools to help you capitalize on both upward and downward movement in stocks, while helping you limit big losses.

In a nutshell, the strategy simultaneously buys and sells put and call options. Of note, bull and bear spreads, often referred to as vertical spreads, but because they limit losses and profits, the strategies should only be used for swing trading movements. There are other bull and bear spread strategies for longer-term position trading, but we will not discuss them here.

This chapter discusses the nuts and bolts behind bull and bear spreads, in terms of swing trading, with actual trading examples and then the risks of bull and bear spreads and how to identify when the timing for bull and bear spreads is not right.

SPREADS: THE NUTS AND BOLTS

As already mentioned, bull and bear spreads are implemented by simultaneously buying and selling put and call options. Here we'll cover how bull spreads work and then move on to bear spreads.

First, though, we need to cover the concept of put-call parity, which is the method of defining a relationship between puts and calls with the same strike price and expiration. At the end of this discussion, you should understand why the methodology of buying and selling identical options holds true; then we'll cover the actual actions of effecting bull and bear spreads.

The put-call parity relationship was identified in 1969 by Hans Stoll, who stated that all puts and calls with the same underlying instrument, strike price, and expiration date must have some sort of identifiable relationship.[1] His theory was first used with European options but has since been widely accepted as a strategy for American options and for creating a delta-neutral portfolio within the arbitrage field.

For the basis of put-call parity here, we will make two assumptions:

- We are using only American options.
- We assume the options will not be exercised before expiration.

With this in mind, the formula for put-call parity is:

$$C + PV(x) = p + s$$

where
$C = $ Present market price of call
$PV(x) = $ Present value of strike (x), less the risk-free rate to expiration[2]
$p = $ Present market price of put
$s = $ Present market price of underlying stock

What the put-call parity relationship is saying is that the present market price for the call plus the present value of the options strike price (minus the interest rate you will pay to hold the stock) equals the present price of the put plus the present price of the underlying stock. In essence, the put-call parity is telling us that a call and cash required to purchase the stock now (discounted for risk-free interest rate to expiration) should equal a put and the underlying stock at expiration.

In essence, put-call parity is what makes bull and bear spreads work, because it generally means that the market (traders and market makers) will price the puts and calls equally in regard to the cash required to hold to expiration and the underlying stock.

You don't need to know how to value options for bull and bear spreads, and the parity relationship does not take into consideration any of the actual underlying option valuation. It is simply the proof we need to understand why we can assume the market generally prices calls and puts at parity all of the time. When calls and puts are not in parity, floor traders quickly take advantage of the situation—smelling an arbitrage opportunity—thus bringing prices back into parity. With so many automated trading systems now in effect within the markets, parity arbitrage opportunities are almost never available—unless, of course, you are a participant in open outcry (the guys on the floor screaming and yelling). For our needs, though, we can assume that put-call parity (upheld by arbitrage-hungry floor traders and fast-acting automated trading systems) simply means we can take on bull and bear spreads without too much worry of the puts and calls not being valued correctly.

The Bull Call Spread

A bull spread is often referred to as a bullish vertical spread strategy and can be created using both calls and puts. Bull call spreads are created by purchasing a call option with a relatively low exercise price, while simultaneously selling a call option with a higher exercise price.

Here's an example: Assume Stock XXX is trading at $50 in January. The February $50 call option is trading at $52, meaning that there is at present $2 of premium (intrinsic value) in the at-the-money February option. At the same time, the January $60 call is trading for 50 cents.

We believe the stock is going up, so we buy one contract (100 shares) of the February $50 for $200 (option price of $2 × one contract of 100 shares = our cost of $200), while selling one contract earning $50 (50 cents × 100 = $50).

Thus, our total cost basis for the trade is $150 (the money we paid for the February $50 calls minus the income we received for selling the February $60 calls).

The trade would be profitable *only* if the stock closes above $51.50, as our gross outlay for the position is $150, with our net outlay being the cost to implement the position plus any transaction fees incurred.

Let's say the stock is trading at $63 a share at the time of expiration. Our profit would be $8.50 per share, or $850 for the total position ($8.50 × 100 shares for our $50 call contract). We can receive a total profit of only $850 because should the stock trade above $60, we would have to hand over the shares we received from buying the $50 calls to the person who bought the $60 calls we wrote. So whenever we implement a bull call spread, our profit is limited to the difference between the intrinsic value of the lower price call option (less the premium we collected) and the strike price of the higher price call option we sold.

Our risk in the trade is the total amount we have paid for the spread, which in this case is $150. Unless we close the position prior to expiration, if the stock closes below $50 a share, we would lose 100 percent of our investment.

However, if the stock closes above $60 a share, our gain would be 567 percent. Mathematically, the gain looks like the $50 call profit ($1,000) minus our cost ($150) = $850. Then, $850/$150 = 567 percent gain.

Let's consider these numbers for a moment, though. If we bought 100 shares of the stock in the open market, we would have to outlay $5,000. If the stock closed at $62 at the time of expiration, we would gain $12 in profit, or $1,200. The total gain in real dollars is more than that of implementing one contract of bull spread, however, in the case of the option spread; we laid out only $150, whereas when we purchased the stock, we had to let $5,000 sit in the market for over a month. Chances are, we could have invested that money somewhere else. What's more, on a percentage basis, assuming the stock closes at $62 a share at expiration, the option position would have returned 567 percent, while the stock position would have only returned 24 percent. What's more, if the stock closed at $45 at the time of expiration in February, we would have lost $150 in the option position, while the stock position would have declined $500. Yes, on a percentage basis, we did lose 100 percent of the option position, but in real dollars, the stock loss would have been 233 percent greater than the options loss.

Really, then, as long as we don't risk too much capital when implementing bull call spreads, we actually increase our percentage return potential while using drastically less capital in the process, all the while limiting our downside risk substantially—in real dollars. The key, though, is not risking too much capital. If we invest all of our money in one trade and the lower price call option expires worthless, our wallets will be empty.

The Bear Put Spread

Bear put spreads are pretty much the same as bull call spreads, except that we are using put options to make money when the stock goes down, not up. Using the same stock price as before, $50 a share, to implement the bear put spread, we would buy a put with a strike above or at where the stock is trading now, and sell the option below where the stock is at present.

Let's assume the February $50 puts are trading for $1.50 and the February $40 puts are selling for 25 cents a share (implying an overall bullish outlook for the stock, as the put prices are below the call prices—meaning those selling call options are demanding a higher premium because the risk is higher). In our example, we would buy one contract (100 shares) of the February put $50 for $1.50, outlaying $150, while simultaneously selling the February $40 put for 25 cents. Our total cost for the position would then be $125.

If the stock traded at $62 at expiration, we would lose our entire investment, as the February put options expire worthless, taking with them the premium we received for selling the lower price put options as well. However, if the stock closed at $39 a share at expiration, we would earn $8.75 for the trade as denoted in the $50 (the strike of the put option we purchased) minus $40 (the put option we sold), less the premium we paid ($125). What we've done is pay $125 to profit $875, which equates to a 700 percent win.

Again, on a percentage basis, the option win (assuming the stock drops below our strike) is substantially higher than just shorting the stock outright, while keeping our real dollar loss very small.

SPREADS IN ACTION

Here's an actual trading example of how spreads work. For our demonstration, we use a bear put spread; however, the same principles apply to a bull call spread.

Our example is BPZ Resources (NYSE: BZP), which is an oil and gas exploration company, engaged in the production and development of natural gas and oil.

Over 2008, the stock witnessed a major rally. Wall Street inferred big bucks on the horizon, as the company continually found—and brought online—more wells from its properties. Thus far, the company has done an incredible job, as seen with the company's insanely low production costs of about $20 per barrel of oil. Investors liked the fact that the company owns about 2.4 million acres of prime oil and gas land in Northwest Peru, and the stock was up just over 100 percent from the start of 2008 to the second week of May.[3]

Here's the thing, though. Although the company is incredible and the outlook is certainly bright, exuberance investors have driven the stock though the roof, based on future expectations. Moreover, as we know from previous chapters, anytime investors begin mindlessly buying overhyped stocks, we—as informed, commonsense, fundamentally sound, and technically savvy swing traders—know a trading opportunity exists.

On a commonsense fundamental level, in the second week of May, the stock was trading with no PE, as the company had yet to produce revenue. But it will, and analysts expected full-year EPS to come in at 70 cents per share, giving the stock (at $24.25 per share) a forward PE of 15.46. While the PE is certainly reasonable, commonsense investors also know the stock is trading with a price to book ratio of 20.33. What's more, as of the second week of May, because the company had no direct income yet, the price to sales ratio was a very high 788.

What we can infer is that over 2008, the market was pricing in exuberance, expecting the company to see positive net income for the first time in the third quarter of 2008. However, as exuberance often commands, all of the stock's current premium is based on future expectations. That leaves much to be desired in the reality of the here and now. Exuberant investors holding the company's proven reserves were priced in, but left out all potential future exploration finds. Again, we're relying heavily on an event in the future that has yet to occur; exactly the scenario that commands exuberance.

The kicker comes from the simple fact that the CFO sold 35,000 shares of stock at the end of March for $21.15. If the outlook for the current year is so darned good, why is the CFO selling stock?[4]

Moreover, common sense tells us that exuberance is expecting the company to perform at peak capacity and is not taking into account the slight possibility of anything going wrong. Also, with the U.S. dollar on the eve of a larger reversal from lows, the company could see lower than expected future profits, should the greenback truly rally. This reasoning is the method we use to find overbought situations and swing trades. When we understand the economics behind the trade, implementing the position is simply a matter of finding the correct strategy and type of instrument with which we can effect the trade.

Simply put, exuberance within this overbought stock opens the door to a swing trade because we are expecting the stock to cool off to a realistic level.

We are not betting that the company isn't incredible and doesn't have a bright future; we are simply betting that, in the short term, exuberant investors have ramped the stock through the roof, which we can capitalize on (Figure 21.1) with a near-term short position clip.

PUT OPTIONS				Expire at close Fri, Jun 20, 2008			
Strike	Symbol	Last	Chg	Bid	Ask	Vol	Open Int
7.50	BZPRU.X	0.40	0.00	N/A	0.10	0	228
10.00	BZPRB.X	0.15	0.00	N/A	0.10	0	151
12.50	BZPRV.X	0.35	0.00	N/A	0.15	0	354
15.00	BZPRC.X	0.10	0.00	N/A	0.10	10	704
17.50	BZPRW.X	0.11	0.00	N/A	0.15	26	1,097
20.00	BZPRD.X	0.35	0.00	0.35	0.50	79	260
22.50	BZPRX.X	1.05	↑ 0.05	1.00	1.15	18	272
25.00	BZPRE.X	2.05	↑ 0.10	2.15	2.35	4	35
30.00	BZPRF.X	6.70	0.00	5.90	6.20	11	11

FIGURE 21.1   BPZ Resources (NYSE: BZP)
Source: Chart courtesy of StockCharts.com

Looking at the company's option June option chain (Figure 21.2), we see that we can implement a bear put spread by purchasing the June $22.50 puts (BZPRX) for $1.05, (Figure 21.3) while simultaneously selling the June $20 puts (BZPRD) for 35 cents.

Our cost basis for the position would be 70 cents per share, or $70 for one contract. Our total loss potential is the entire $70, if exuberance continues and the stock does not decline before the June expiration on Friday, June 20.

However, our total gain potential would be $1.80 ($22.50 − $20 = $2.50 − $0.70 = $1.80). With our cost at 70 cents, the total trade percentage gain potential equals 257 percent, or $180 a share.

What's important to remember is this:

- On June 20 (expiration), the stock would have to be trading below $20 per share for us to hit our maximum profit potential.
- If the stock trades above $22.50 at expiration, we lose 100 percent of our investment.

Here's why this strategy is great for swing traders. If we wanted to short 100 shares of stock, we would have to invest $2,422 dollars. If the stock does fall below $20 a share at expiration, it is true we would miss $2.42 in profit ($4.22 − $1.80 = $2.42), translating to total missed money of $242. However, keep in mind that we invested a mere $70 in the options strategy, versus more than two grand to actually hold the stock short. What's more, if the stock rips upward to $30, with the options strategy, we limit our losses to $70, while by holding the stock we would have lost $578.

PUT OPTIONS								Expire at close Fri, Jun 20, 2008
Strike	Symbol	Last	Chg	Bid	Ask	Vol	Open Int	
7.5	BZPRU.X	0.4	0	N/A	0.15	0	228	
10	BZPRB.X	0.05	0	N/A	N/A	1	150	
12.5	BZPRV.X	0.05	0	N/A	0.15	10	354	
15	BZPRC.X	0.1	0	N/A	0.15	10	704	
17.5	BZPRW.X	0.05	0	N/A	0.15	10	1,058	
20	BZPRD.X	0.15	0	0.05	0.15	6	421	
22.5	BZPRX.X	0.4 ↓	0.35	0.3	0.4	1	1,347	
25	BZPRE.X	1.9 ↓	0.25	1.35	1.45	62	367	
30	BZPRF.X	6.8 ↑	0.3	5.7	6	10	21	
								Highlighted options are in-the-money.

FIGURE 21.2 BZP Options Chain
Source: Chart courtesy of StockCharts.com

FIGURE 21.3 BPZ Resources Bear Spread Setup (NYSE: BZP)
Source: Chart courtesy of StockCharts.com

The point of the above example is twofold. First, one of the greatest
lessons I've (Whistler) learned as an options trader is *always* give your
position more time than you think to move. If you think the position will
move in one month, give it three. If you think it will move in three, give it
six. Here's why, when trading options, if the underlying stock has not made
a move before expiration, we stand to lose everything. And in options,
when expiration approaches, the contract will quickly lose value—don't
forget—the guys who write options want to keep the premium you paid
them. In the case of BPZ Resources, the stock continued to fire up to highs
throughout almost all of June, partially fueled by the incessant promotion
of Jim Cramer on Mad Money. However, in July, when oil fell from highs,
BPZ Resources was crushed. And by August, it had lost almost 50% of its
value from highs just one month earlier. Option traders who were expecting a downward move, but did not give themselves enough time (in terms
of expiration) lost everything, just before the trade would have made a

fortune. Also, don't forget that all of the people who were buying high—based on the exuberant media frenzy that surrounded the stock—were crushed too. Please, don't be a sucker.

In all, we certainly hope this chapter has shown how using options spreads can dramatically improve the swing trader's bottom line, while minimizing risk at the same time.

Remember that options carry an immense amount of risk, as shown in the large loss potential in this chapter. However, the losses are only as large as the money invested, so the final point of this chapter is to tell you to *never* overextend yourself with options. Because the gain potential is so high, you really need to invest only 10 percent of the capital you would have used if you had bought or sold the actual stock itself. By doing so, we protect ourselves from unforeseen whopper losses and give ourselves an incredible win opportunity, all at the same time.

LAST WORDS

We would like to take a moment to thank every reader for your support; we hope that this book will help you in your investing pursuits not only in the short term but for many, many years to come.

With this, we would also like to add that if there is one point from this entire book that we would like to impress on you, it's using common sense when investing. So many people begin investing in the highest spirits. Eventually, their feelings of elation can dwindle, especially if the market presents difficult conditions. However, it is at these moments that common sense will always prevail. Simply taking the time to step back from the market—even if you're winning—and look at things from a distance can save the day. When we take a moment to remove ourselves from the situation and clear our minds, common sense can come to us like a life preserver in the middle of a whitewater river.

So many swap common sense for fear or greed. And really why not, given that fear and greed are everything that drives markets? But there's a different paradigm of approaching the market available to those who wish to see clearly.

Remember that things are never as good as they seem when stocks are hitting new highs and the euphoria is out of control. On the flip side, when everyone from the media to your peers is giving up on the stock market, it is not the end of the world. The feelings of great desperation that bring thoughts of cashing out all your accounts and burying your dollars in a hole in the backyard are not rational. Again, this goes back to common sense.

Granted, we are all humans, and emotions and irrational thoughts about the market are natural, but when they occur, it is time to step away from the computer for a day to refocus your attention. We hope this book could be a solace for you to turn to in times of heightened emotions. Flipping through the strategies that have worked well for swing traders and will work again for you can bring you new insights, and by sticking with the plan, long-term success will be yours.

Best of luck!

Notes

Chapter 1   Determining Your Trading Style

1. BrainyQuote.com: Ibsen, Henrick. Accessed May 2008 at http://www.brainyquote.com/quotes/authors/h/henrik_ibsen.html.
2. "What Warren Thinks. . . ." *Forbes* magazine, April 14, 2008. Accessed April 2008 at http://money.cnn.com/galleries/2008/fortune/0804/gallery.buffett.fortune/index.html?cnn=yes.

Chapter 2   The First Rule of Profitability: Stop Loss

1. Salmon, Felix. "The Bear Facts." Condé Nast Portfolio.com, March 14, 2008. Accessed April 2008 at http://www.portfolio.com/news-markets/top-5/2008/03/14/The-Bear-Facts.
2. Zarroli, Jim. "Fed's Bear Stearns Move Breaks New Ground." NPR *All Things Considered*, March 17, 2008. Accessed April 2008 at http://www.npr.org/templates/story/story.php?storyId=88415067.

Chapter 4   The Third Rule of Profitability: Technical Analysis

1. John J. Murphy. *Technical Analysis of the Financial Markets* (Upper Saddle River, NJ: Prentice Hall, 1999).

Chapter 5   Strategy 1: Take the Trends to Pieces

1. Note for the purposes of this example, in the first period EMA calculation, Day 1 Close Price was used as the Previous EMA (PEMA).

Chapter 8 Strategy 4: The Tier II Play

1. "The Home Depot Announces Fourth Quarter and Fiscal 2007 Results; Provides Fiscal 2008 Outlook." Accessed April 2008 at http://biz.yahoo.com/prnews/080226/cltu033a.html?.v=1.

Chapter 9 Strategy 5: ETF Sector Rotation

1. See http://www.forextheory.com/technical-analysis/dow-theory.html. Accessed July 2008.
2. Chad Langager and Casey Murphy. "Dow Theory: The Three-Trend Market." *Investopedia*. Accessed July 2008 at http://www.investopedia.com/university/Dowtheory/Dowtheory2.asp.

Chapter 14 Strategy 10: Piggyback Strategy Using ETFs and Mutual Funds

1. Thomas P. McGuigan. "The Difficulty of Selecting Superior Mutual Fund Performance." *Journal of Financial Planning*, February 2006.

Chapter 15 Strategy 11: Scanning for Swing Trade Ideas

1. Investopedia.com.

Chapter 17 Strategy 13: Swing Trading the Megatrends

1. Howard W. French and Lydia Polgreen. "Chinese Flocking in Numbers to a New Frontier: Africa." *International Herald Tribune*, August 17, 2007. Accessed July 2008 at http://www.iht.com/articles/2007/08/17/africa/malawi.php.

Chapter 21 Strategy 17: Bull and Bear Spreads

1. Hans R. Stoll. "The Relationship between Put and Call Option Prices." *Journal of Finance*, 23 (1969), 801–824.
2. Risk Free Rate = Usually defined as the potential interest that could be earned on three-month U.S. Treasury bills, which are generally thought of as one of the safest investments in the world.

3. Form 10-Q for BPZ RESOURCES, INC. Accessed May 2008 at http://biz.yahoo.com/e/080509/bzp10-q.html.

4. BPZ Resources CFO Sells Shares, Wednesday April 2, 2:07 pm ET http://biz.yahoo.com/ap/080402/bpz_resources_caminos_insider_trans actions.html?.v=1.

Bibliography

Bernstein, William. *The Four Pillars of Investing* (New York: McGraw Hill, 2002).

Black, Fischer. "The Holes in Black-Scholes," *Risk*, March 1988, pp. 30–32.

Black, Fisher. "Living Up to the Model," *Risk*, March 1990, pp. 11–13.

Bookstaber, Richard, *Option Pricing and Investment Strategies*, 3rd ed. (Chicago: Probus Publishing, 1991).

Crane, John. *Advanced Swing Trading: Strategies to Predict, Identify, and Trade Future Market Swings* (New York: John Wiley & Sons, 2004).

Graham, Benjamin. *The Intelligent Investor* (1949; reprint, New York: HarperCollins, 2005).

Hale, Timothy. *Smarter Investing—Simpler Decisions for Better Results* (New York: Prentice Hall, 2006).

Hulbert, Mark. "Buy and Hold? Sure, but Don't Forget the Hold," *New York Times*, July 2, 2006.

Luft, Carl, and Richard Sheiner. *Understanding and Trading Listed Stock Options* (Chicago: Probus Publishing, 1988).

Mauboussin, Michael. *More Than You Know: Finding Financial Wisdom in Unconventional Places* (New York: Columbia University Press, 2006).

McMillan, Lawrence. *Options as a Strategic Investment: A Comprehensive Analysis of Listed Option Strategies*, 3rd ed. (New York: New York Institute of Finance, 1993).

Murphy, John. *Technical Analysis of the Financial Markets: A Comprehensive Guide toTrading Methods and Applications* (New York: New York Institute of Finance, 1999).

Natenberg, Sheldon. *Option Volatility and Pricing* (London: Probus Publishing, 1994).

Nison, Steve. *The Candlestick Course*, (New York: John Wiley & Sons 2003).

Pring, Martin. *Technical Analysis Explained: The Successful Investor's Guide to Spotting Investment Trends and Turning Points*, 3rd ed. (McGraw Hill 1991).

Whistler, Mark. *Trade with Passion and Purpose, Spiritual, Psychological and Philosophical Keys to Becoming a Top Trader* (New York: John Wiley & Sons, 2007).

Whistler, Mark. *Trading Pairs, Capturing Profits and Hedging Risk with Statistical Arbitrage Strategies* (New York: John Wiley & Sons, 2007).

Zweig, Jason, Ed. *Benjamin Graham, The Intelligent Investor* (1949; reprint, New York: HarperCollins, 2003).

Index